THE SOCIETY OF ILLUSTRATORS
37TH ANNUAL OF AMERICAN ILLUSTRATION
ILLUSTRATORS 37

From the exhibition held in the galleries of the
Society of Illustrators Museum of American Illustration
128 East 63rd Street, New York City
February 11 - April 15, 1995

Society of Illustrators, Inc.
128 East 63rd Street, New York, NY 10021

Copyright© 1995 by Society of Illustrators
All rights reserved. Copyright under International and
Pan-American Copyright Conventions.

No part of this book may be reproduced, stored in a retrieval system or transmitted in any
other form, or by any means, electronic, mechanical, photocopying, recording or
otherwise, without prior permission of the publishers.

While the Society of Illustrators makes every effort possible to publish full and correct
credits for each work included in this volume, sometimes errors of omission or
commission may occur. For this the Society is most regretful, but hereby must disclaim
any liability.

As this book is printed in four-color process, a few of the illustrations reproduced here
may appear to be slightly different than in their original reproduction.

ISBN 0-8230-6415-8
Library of Congress Catalog Card Number 59-10849

Distributors to the trade in the United States
Watson-Guptill Publications
1515 Broadway, New York, NY 10036

Distributed throughout the rest of the world by:
Rotovision, S.A.
9 Route Suisse
1295 Mies, Switzerland

Edited by Jill Bossert
Cover painting by Gary Kelley
Cover design by Louise Fili, Louise Fili, Ltd.
Interior design by Doug Johnson and Ryuichi Minakawa
Layout and Typesetting by Naomi Minakawa

Printed in Singapore by Provision Pte Ltd.
Tel. 0065-334 7720
Fax: 0065-334 7721

Photo Credits: Mike Benny by Linda Klotz, Harvey Dinnerstein self-portrait, Blair Drawson by Jim Allen, Louise Fili by Gary Kelley,
Colin Forbes by Sally Andersen-Bruce, Mirko Ilic by Poul Hans Lange, Gary Kelley by Murray Tinkelman,
Richard Merkin by Valentine Sheldon, Frank Metz by Simon Metz, Rafal Olbinski by Czeslaw Czaplinski,
C.F. Payne by Alan Brown/Photonics Graphics, Jessica Weber by Henry Grossman

Published by Rotovision S.A. Geneva

PRESIDENT'S MESSAGE

Welcome to what I know you will agree is a very comfortable book.

Each volume of the Illustrators Annual brings to us the familiar images of the best of illustration today. Both the regulars and the newcomers speak in friendly tones about the perseverance it took to reach these pages; they also speak about the satisfaction this professional recognition gives them.

These artists are like family. Their art tells stories oft repeated and gladly listened to again and again, like the joke you enjoy even more the second time you hear it.

Wilson McLean chaired the 37th Annual. Marshall Arisman was his assistant. They're a couple of major talents who took the time to create a great show and this book. Thanks, gents.

So sit back in your Laz-E-Boy and say hello to some good friends.

Peter Fiore
President
1993 - 1995

Portrait by Daniel Schwartz

EXECUTIVE OFFICERS 1994-1995

HONORARY PRESIDENT / *Stevan Dohanos (1906-1994)*
PRESIDENT / *Peter Fiore*
EXECUTIVE VICE PRESIDENT / *Vincent Di Fate*
VICE PRESIDENT / *Steven Stroud*
TREASURER / *Dean Ellis*
ASSOCIATE TREASURER / *Richard Berenson*
SECRETARY / *Dennis Lyall*
HOUSE CHAIRMAN / *Al Lorenz*

BOARD OF DIRECTORS 1994-1995

ADVISORY / *Shannon Stirnweis*
ANNUAL EXHIBITION / *Wilson McLean*
BULLETIN / *Jon Weiman*
CHRISTMAS AUCTION / *Everett Davidson*
HOLIDAY FUND / *Eileen Hedy Schultz*
COMMUNITY SERVICE / *Judy Francis*
EDUCATION / *Alvin J. Pimsler*
EXTENDED MEMBERSHIP / *Eric Fowler*
FINANCE / *Dean Ellis*
FUND DEVELOPMENT / *Richard Berenson*
GALLERY (HANGING) / *Steve Cieslawski*
GOVERNMENT SERVICE / *Gil Cohen, Keith Ferris (Honorary)*
GRAPHICS / *Richard Berenson*
HALL OF FAME / *Murray Tinkelman, Willis Pyle (Emeritus)*
HOUSE / *Al Lorenz*
INSTRUCTION / *Barbara Carr*
INTERNATIONAL / *Barbara Carr*
LECTURE SERIES / *Joel Iskowitz*
LEGISLATION / *Carol Donner*
LIFE/SENIOR MEMBERSHIP / *Dean Ellis*
MEMBERSHIP / *Dennis Dittrich*
MEMBERS GALLERY / *Mitchell Hooks*
MUSEUM / *Dennis Lyall*
PERMANENT COLLECTION / *Vincent Di Fate, Doreen Minuto*
PROFESSIONAL PRACTICES (JOINT ETHICS COMMITTEE) / *Nancy Lou Makris*
PUBLICATIONS / *Gerald McConnell*
SPECIAL EVENTS / *Emma Crawford*
WELFARE / *Dean Ellis*

37TH ANNUAL EXHIBITION COMMITTEE

CHAIRMAN, *Wilson McLean*
ASSISTANT CHAIRMAN, *Marshall Arisman*
POSTER ILLUSTRATOR, *Etienne Delessert*
POSTER DESIGNER, *Rita Marshall*
GALLERY (HANGING) COMMITTEE, *Steve Cieslawski*
PHOTOGRAPHY, *Steven Green-Armytage*
GALA INVITATION DESIGNER, *Anthony Russell*

SI STAFF

DIRECTOR, *Terrence Brown*
ASSISTANT DIRECTOR, *Phyllis Harvey*
HOUSE MANAGER, *Michael Sysyn*
CATERING, *Karlton Harris*
STAFF AND OTHER HELPERS, *Patrick Arrasmith*
Bea Brass
Catherine Citarella Brown
Karen Charatan
Allen Douglas
Anna Lee Fuchs
Michael Mancuso
Nancy Starosky
Donna Sysyn
Rena Tomashefsky
Janet Weithas

ILLUSTRATORS 37 ANNUAL BOOK

EDITOR, *Jill Bossert*
INTERIOR DESIGN, *Doug Johnson, Ryuichi Minakawa*
COVER DESIGN, *Louise Fili, Louise Fili, Ltd.*
COVER PAINTING, *Gary Kelley*
LAYOUT AND TYPESETTING, *Naomi Minakawa, Minakawa Design*

THE SOCIETY OF ILLUSTRATORS AWARDS

Since 1958, the Society of Illustrators has elected to its Hall of Fame artists recognized for their "distinguished achievement in the art of illustration." The list of previous winners is truly a "Who's Who" of illustration. Former Presidents of the Society meet annually to elect those who will be so honored.

The Hamilton King Award, created by Mrs. Hamilton King in memory of her husband through a bequest, is presented annually for the best illustration of the year by a member of the Society. The selection is made by former recipients of this award and may be won only once.

Also, the Society of Illustrators presents Special Awards each year for substantial contributions to the profession. The Dean Cornwell Recognition Award honors someone for past service which has proven to have been an important contribution to the Society. The Arthur William Brown Achievement Award honors someone who has made a substantial contribution to the Society over a period of time.

HALL OF FAME LAUREATES 1995
James Avati
McClelland Barclay*
Joseph Clement Coll*
Frank E. Schoonover*

HAMILTON KING AWARD 1965-1995

Paul Calle 1965	Gerald McConnell 1981
Bernie Fuchs 1966	Robert Heindel 1982
Mark English 1967	Robert M. Cunningham 1983
Robert Peak 1968	Braldt Bralds 1984
Alan E. Cober 1969	Attila Hejja 1985
Ray Ameijide 1970	Doug Johnson 1986
Miriam Schottland 1971	Kinuko Y. Craft 1987
Charles Santore 1972	James McMullan 1988
Dave Blossom 1973	Guy Billout 1989
Fred Otnes 1974	Edward Sorel 1990
Carol Anthony 1975	Brad Holland 1991
Judith Jampel 1976	Gary Kelley 1992
Leo & Diane Dillon 1977	Jerry Pinkney 1993
Daniel Schwartz 1978	John Collier 1994
William Teason 1979	C.F. Payne 1995
Wilson McLean 1980	

HALL OF FAME LAUREATES 1958-1994

Norman Rockwell 1958	Stan Galli 1981
Dean Cornwell 1959	Frederic R. Gruger* 1981
Harold Von Schmidt 1959	John Gannam* 1981
Fred Cooper 1960	John Clymer 1982
Floyd Davis 1961	Henry P. Raleigh* 1982
Edward Wilson 1962	Eric (Carl Erickson)* 1982
Walter Biggs 1963	Mark English 1983
Arthur William Brown 1964	Noel Sickles* 1983
Al Parker 1965	Franklin Booth* 1983
Al Dorne 1966	Neysa Moran McMein* 1984
Robert Fawcett 1967	John LaGatta* 1984
Peter Helck 1968	James Williamson* 1984
Austin Briggs 1969	Charles Marion Russell* 1985
Rube Goldberg 1970	Arthur Burdett Frost* 1985
Stevan Dohanos 1971	Robert Weaver 1985
Ray Prohaska 1972	Rockwell Kent* 1986
Jon Whitcomb 1973	Al Hirschfeld 1986
Tom Lovell 1974	Haddon Sundblom* 1987
Charles Dana Gibson* 1974	Maurice Sendak 1987
N.C. Wyeth* 1974	René Bouché* 1988
Bernie Fuchs 1975	Pruett Carter* 1988
Maxfield Parrish* 1975	Robert T. McCall 1988
Howard Pyle* 1975	Erté 1989
John Falter 1976	John Held Jr. 1989*
Winslow Homer* 1976	Arthur Ignatius Keller 1989*
Harvey Dunn* 1976	Burt Silverman 1990
Robert Peak 1977	Robert Riggs* 1990
Wallace Morgan* 1977	Morton Roberts* 1990
J.C. Leyendecker* 1977	Donald Teague 1991
Coby Whitmore 1978	Jessie Willcox Smith* 1991
Norman Price* 1978	William A. Smith* 1991
Frederic Remington* 1978	Joe Bowler 1992
Ben Stahl 1979	Edwin A. Georgi* 1992
Edwin Austin Abbey* 1979	Dorothy Hood* 1992
Lorraine Fox* 1979	Robert McGinnis 1993
Saul Tepper 1980	Thomas Nast* 1993
Howard Chandler Christy* 1980	Coles Phillips* 1993
James Montgomery Flagg* 1980	Harry Anderson 1994
	Elizabeth Shippen Green* 1994
	Ben Shahn* 1994

*Presented posthumously

HALL OF FAME COMMITTEE 1995
CHAIRMAN, Murray Tinkelman
CHAIRMAN EMERITUS, Willis Pyle
FORMER PRESIDENTS
  Diane Dillon, Charles McVicker, Wendell Minor, Howard Munce, Alvin J. Pimsler, Warren Rogers, Eileen Hedy Schultz, Shannon Stirnweis, David K. Stone, John Witt

HALL OF FAME 1995
James Avati *b. 1912*

As in Giotto's intimate bible scenes, James Avati sets a small stage upon which the story is acted out. His pictures are not illustrations of the words of a text, but encapsulations of the theme. Each character remains stubbornly and uniquely individual. Placed intimately together in a small room, in a folk culture, at a certain hour and season, his characters act out the ordeals of everyday life. Their bodies and faces confess, the disarray of their costumes reveals, the clutter on the bed testifies, the remnants of a meal are evidence, and the other side of the tracks through the window sets the scene so that we can see the story happening ourselves. We forget that it is Avati who is making it take place.

Norman Rockwell painted us as we would like to see ourselves—at our best. Avati is the flip side of Rockwell. He is also on the other side of a trend toward abstraction, self-expression, and retreat from content which characterized the post-World War II years. Avati is no rebel or Social Realist, but rather a Naturalist, painting us with our suspenders down.

Avati, like many back from the war, was no longer exactly young, but he had no formal training and had no bad habits as a "schlock-artist" to overcome. His standards had been set during his studies at Mercer and Princeton University. His father was a society portrait photographer and he married the daughter of an artist and an art director, who were both at the top of their fields. Like other soldiers back from the hard truths of a real war, he was ambitious to work at the most serious levels possible. From 1949 he produced work for *Collier's*, *American* magazine, *McCall's*, and *The Atlantic Monthly*, among others.

The strong mass market appeal of paperback books, with their stories distilled on the covers, was a post-war phenomenon. The books were written by the great authors of the day, color printing had become cheap, and television had not yet arrived. Also, the advertising-filled magazines were designed to sell dreams of gluttony after a long spell of hard times and shortages.

New paperback companies did not have to satisfy old readerships; their readers were fresh, young, and literate. There was no traditional visual form to follow. Of course, the "pulps" were folded in as compost and some covers were designed as trash, but for new books there was much experimentation with fresh imagery. The best writers, coupled with the new paperback venue for serious pictures, gave beginners like Avati a chance.

Avati at work on a Pocketbook cover in Red Bank, New Jersey, 1953

It was a very small window of opportunity—perhaps a dozen year—until the business was overwhelmed by TV, mall marketing, and art directors fighting for rack space. It was high noon for low kitsch, yet in those years, Avati created some masterpieces of American illustration.

Avati's pictures contain characterizations and narratives more powerful than the usual humorous, moralizing, and condescending comedies of genre painting. His pictures are as serious in intent as the writing they illustrated. Sometimes they are in the burlesque mode, as in Erskine Caldwell's Southland; sometimes in the tragic vein of William Faulkner's deep South; sometimes of the brutal vitality of John Farrell's Chicago in the depression years. Sometimes they display white American males coming to terms with other sexualities, races, and cultures, as in Ralph Ellison's invisible Black or Pearl Buck's Chinese. Most often it is the intense relations between men and women regardless of time, place, race, or class, which are Avati's subjects.

Avati was born in and lived most of his life in Red Bank, New Jersey. When he was nearly 80 years old, he left his second family and pursued the woman he loved to Petaluma, California, taking with him one of his sons, his ninth child. This journey was as strange as any he illustrated on a paperback cover.

But it was in Red Bank that he found his types and settings. His models are real people from the neighborhood who peer out at us with both shyness and self-liberation as they find themselves in a cameo part in one of Avati's fictional dramas. Their awkwardness is endearing, their commonness, beautiful.

Avati's people live in that homely corner from which we ascend to reach the world of Culture, Counter Culture, Patriotic idealism, the expression of agonized Genius, Religious Awe, or Masterpieces. That's not where Avati is; Avati works deep inside our private opinion about what the world is actually like. We aren't all that good, or all that bad, or all that picturesque. We are all Avati characters.

Stanley Meltzoff

HALL OF FAME 1995
McClelland Barclay (1893-1943)

Although he achieved widespread fame for his paintings of beautiful women, McClelland Barclay was an artist with many interests who painted a variety of subjects. His first love was the sea, a passion that permeated his whole life. Barclay's earliest artwork was marine and as a young man he spent time as a sailor and fisherman before working for the Federal Bureau of Fisheries as a collector. One of his favorite retreats was Monhegan Island in Maine where he did a number of paintings of the sea.

Born in St. Louis, Missouri, Barclay studied art at the St. Louis Museum of Fine Arts; the Corcoran Gallery of Art in Washington, D.C.; the Art Students League in New York City; and the Chicago Art Institute. He later became a member of the Society of Illustrators and was one of the founding members of the Artist's Guild of Chicago. Barclay began his commercial art career in Chicago, and then became allied with the McManus Agency in Detroit. In 1921 he created the advertising campaign which would garner him widespread recognition: the girl with the "Body By Fisher" for General Motors. This very successful campaign extended into the early 1930s. The ads were reproduced in magazines and on billboards, and most followed the same format: full-color images of two or three figures, outlined in black, silhouetted on white ground. Barclay favored bright primary colors: blues, reds, yellows, and oranges, making these paintings bold and eye-catching. The Fisher Body Girl was sophisticated and beautifully dressed, as were the girls he painted for magazine covers and story illustrations for *Redbook*, *Cosmopolitan*, *The Saturday Evening Post*, and *Ladies' Home Journal*, among others, and ads for many other clients.

In 1933 Barclay gave his girls more curves, rounding out the long and lean figure of the Fisher Body Girl. His new subjects were more apt to be engaged in sports, mirroring his own interests in horseback riding, water and snow skiing, and tennis. At the same time, his painting style evolved into a less hard-edged and more painterly one; the brush strokes became shorter and less blended.

Barclay's commercial illustration subjects were not limited to fashionable girls. He painted for industrial clients including the Koppers Company, who manufactured machinery; Camel cigarettes; Texaco, and Mobil Oil. In 1939 he established the McClelland Barclay Art Products Corporation which produced a myriad of objects, all of which he designed and sculpted. They included sterling silver and costume jewelry, cast metal bookends, ashtrays, boxes, lamps, vases, and plaques. These were generally ornamented with subjects from nature: leaves, flowers, birds, and animals.

Patriotism was another defining characteristic of Barclay's life. During both world wars he created numerous prize-winning recruiting posters for the military and for the Red Cross. In World War I, he worked for the United States Shipping Board, where he was involved with the design and implementation of camouflage for troop transports and commercial vessels.

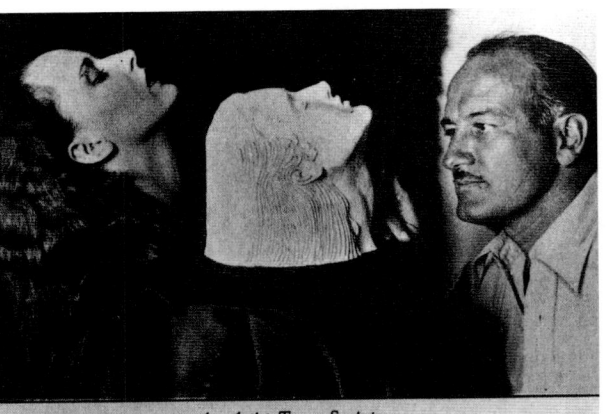

An Artist Turns Sculptor
McClelland Barclay, passing a vacation in Havana, changes from canvas to clay and models a head of his wife, who has posed for many of his paintings. *Associated Press*

In 1938 Barclay joined the United States Navy, believing that America would enter the war in Europe against Germany. As a member of the first unit of the War Arts Corps, he wanted to paint military action as it truly was, to create a permanent historical record of the war. He consequently traveled extensively and painted enlisted men as well as the leading American military officers including Generals Marshall and MacArthur (whose portrait he completed in Australia), and Admirals Nimitz, King, and Halsey. Barclay loved the Pacific, particularly Hawaii, and had planned to settle there after the war to paint portraits and marine scenes. He was reported missing in action on a torpedoed L.S.T. in the Solomon Sea two weeks before his scheduled return home.

Lieutenant Commander McClelland Barclay was posthumously awarded the Purple Heart in 1944. Also in 1944, an illustration he did for Koppers was honored with the Art Directors Club Medal. He was cited "in recognition of his long and distinguished record in editorial illustration and advertising art, and in honor of his devotion and meritorious service to his county as a commissioned officer in the United States Navy which lists him as missing in action in the South Pacific." In 1946 on the third anniversary of his death, a foundation in his name was established. Implemented through grants to leading art schools and gallery exhibits of original paintings, the McClelland Barclay Fund For Art was formed "to aid thousands of American artists who never had a fair opportunity to market their work."

Judy Francis

"At the Station," a 1931 Body by Fisher advertisement, oil on panel. Private collection.

HALL OF FAME 1995
Joseph Clement Coll *(1881-1921)*

Joseph Clement Coll's greatest admirers during his lifetime—and since—have been his fellow illustrators. For much of his career, beginning in 1905, he labored in the relative obscurity of a Sunday newspaper supplement, the *Associated Sunday Magazines*.

Over the next ten years he evolved into one of America's finest practitioners in the medium of pen and ink. His own heroes were Edwin Austin Abbey and the Spanish master, Daniel Vierge, and he rivaled them both in skill. Coll was unrivaled in his unique vision, however, and in the imagination of his pictorial concepts. Perhaps it grew out of his Irish heritage. Certainly it was nurtured by the many Irish stories he illustrated by the authors Seumas MacManus and Maude Radford Warren, as well as the fantastic novel, *The Lost World* by Sir Arthur Conan Doyle, which Coll copiously illustrated in serialized form for the *Associated Sunday Magazines* over a period of several months.

His most evocative illustrations were done for an extensive series of short stories published in *Collier's* magazine about the mysterious Dr. Fu Manchu by the author Sax Rohmer. The stories had everything—high adventure, intrigue, sex, and the shadowy menace of a diabolical genius aspiring to take control over the Western World. Coll reveled in the freedom of interpretation afforded and chose unusual vantage points and compositional devices that were well ahead of his time.

Although Coll used models and made careful studies from them to aid his renderings, their poses could have been conceptualized only in his head. In working out his picture ideas, he was completely absorbed. His daughter remembered that he would sit in his favorite rocking chair with a blanket over his head to shut out any distractions; and he was not to be disturbed.

Some of Coll's studies survive in the form of warm-up sheets. Like a baseball player or a musician, he would precede his final rendering with exercises of pen strokes of various weights and spacing as well as portions of a head or folds of clothing to coordinate his hand and eye. Certainly the final renderings are virtuoso masterpieces. He could use the pen point like a brush, playing the finest lines against solid blacks.

Coll had begun his short career (he died at forty from appendicitis) as a young apprentice in the newspaper art department of the *New York American*. There he worked his way up from drawing borders and spots to inking portraits over silver prints (early halftones did not reproduce well on newsprint stock) and then on to reportorial assignments. It was basic training for him and he was sent to their Chicago paper for further development. Especially good at rendering figures, he was soon hired by the newly formed *North American* in Philadelphia.

His precocious skill was recognized by a perceptive art director, J. Thomson Willing, who nurtured his career and who sometimes collaborated with him when lettering was needed, as in another Conan Doyle serial, "Sir Nigel a Companion to the White Company." It was Willing who wrote this moving tribute to Coll in *The Century Magazine*, May 1922:

> The boy who did his imaginative work—and
> we who knew him always thought of him as
> a boy destined to do yet bigger things—
> passed away in late October, a loss to the
> art and culture of his time.
> No bargainer for wealth or fame,
> His was the better part—
> A simple love of all his kind,
> And lifelong fervor in his art.

Walt Reed
Illustration House

"Mephisto," from the "Fu Manchu" stories by Sax Rohmer as reproduced in *Collier's*, pen and ink. Permanent Collection of the Society of Illustrators Museum of American Illustration.

HALL OF FAME 1995
Frank E. Schoonover (1877-1972)

Frank E. Schoonover's remarkable career spanned nearly the entire period from 1890 to 1940 affectionately referred to as the "Golden Age of American Illustration." The most capable and best trained of the young artists of the period had studied under the extraordinary tutelage of Howard Pyle, without question one of the greatest contributors to American art and literature.

Despite an inclination to enter the ministry after schooling in Trenton, New Jersey, Schoonover, inspired by a summer advertisement in the *Philadelphia Inquirer*, applied for Pyle's composition class at Drexel Institute in 1896 where he matured substantially, becoming one of the chosen ten for the coveted Pyle summer class in Chadds Ford. Four years later, Pyle handed Schoonover his first commercial assignment. "I was the happiest boy in the world when Mr. Pyle gave me that manuscript."

Thus began 40 years of dedication to a craft that resulted in over 2,000 published images for over 120 books and numerous magazines and periodicals. There were also several long trips as Schoonover strove to experience for himself the emotions of these unique narrative paintings he would later render. It was Pyle who championed the "mental projection," as he called it, in combination with historical fidelity to the subject matter, so that the pictorial story telling would be endowed with a soul unique to the moment portrayed. As his work evolved from 1900 on, we can evaluate his paintings by observing each decade as a chapter in his artistic portfolio.

Schoonover numbered his first illustration for the book, *Jersey Boy in the Revolution*, #1. The date, article, publisher, medium, size, times, models, and even costs were faithfully recorded in his "daybook" continuously through illustration #2,500. If we include the year 1911, the first decade witnessed 500 illustrations; travels to Canada, Montana, New Orleans; and several stories. During the winter trip of 1903 to Hudson Bay, the Objibwa tribe made him a blood brother and anointed him, "Misanagan," or picture-making man. The expenditure of all this energy and inspiration resulted in arguably his finest work: canvases that emote passion and drama, embellished by a palette true to Pyle's teachings—blends of umber, ochre, ultramarine, viridian—earth colors playing light and shadow masterfully throughout the picture.

Pyle's death in November of 1911, boldly noted in Schoonover's daybook, was in some ways the high-water mark for many of the Pyle students. Clearly, Schoonover felt the loss, but with his work in strong demand, he again rendered 500 images, including 24 illustrated books, from 1911 to 1920. The decade ended with a very important series of World War I paintings for *Ladies' Home Journal*. Though mildly romanticized, they were large canvases, occupied with detail, portraying both the guts and the glory of a war. He became a combat artist in abstentia. Fortunately, today all nine paintings hang together in the Delaware State Armory.

During the third decade, Schoonover took on the mantle of children's book illustrator that popularizes him today. Though not as bold as his contemporary, N.C. Wyeth, who worked for Scribner's, Schoonover's covers for *Robin Hood*, *Treasure Island*, *Kidnapped*, and many others published by Harpers, evoke warmth and gentleness very appropriate for the youth of those days. In fact, we count 60 books about cowboys, pirates, presidents, folk heroes, and Knights of the Round Table embellished with almost 800 Schoonover illustrations. This was the wonderful visual playground for a whole generation.

The beginning of the 1930s marks the gradual decline in the role of illustration, though at 53, Schoonover continued to prosper, illustrating another 22 books, and closing out the decade with almost 2,300 paintings. Many of his magazine assignments came from *Country Gentleman* and *American Boy*, neither high-quality publications. Consequently, Schoonover adapted a tri-color palette with various combinations of blue, white, yellow, red, and black, while also vignetting many compositions. Interestingly, his most notable efforts can be found at Emmanuel Episcopal Church: 13 magnificent stained glass windows combine all his illustrative talents in a very spiritual motif. He also painted his only mural in 1939 for the H. Fletcher Brown Vocational School.

Several daybook entries in 1936 acknowledge Schoonover's transition from dedicated illustrator to easel painter: four landscape paintings of Bushkill, Pennsylvania, where he spent his summers at the family home, with a barn/studio just across the stream; "the Land of His Forefathers," as he aptly titled one of his later landscapes. From 1941, he spent the rest of his life recording the lay of the land in the Brandywine and Delaware River valleys. These approximately 200 paintings constitute his artistic epilogue. Many were painted directly over old illustrations whose use became, sadly, stretched canvas. Though he sold some of his works, he prefaced the transaction with the comment, "Why would I want to sell it when I've already been paid for it?"

Schoonover died in 1972 at age 95, having outlived almost all of his contemporaries. His contributions to the heritage of American art, as well as those of many other illustrators, deserve recognition in any analysis of the cultural history of this country. His studios in Wilmington, now restored and open to the public, serve as a living museum and conservation gallery. His election to the Society of Illustrators Hall of Fame finally expresses a professional gratitude for his gift of storytelling images.

John Randall Schoonover
President, Schoonover Studios Ltd.

"A Lone Hand," oil on canvas.

HAMILTON KING AWARD 1995
C.F. Payne b. 1954

I first met Chris at a Society function and quickly discovered that his conversation was as varied and polished as his work. We moved from topic to topic and there just didn't seem to be an area that Chris did not know or care deeply about. We jumped from sports to politics, with occasional forays into bizarre trivia, primarily concerning old TV shows. After that first encounter some years ago, we began telephoning each other on a weekly basis.

Chris's work became a fixture in the Society's Annuals about a dozen years ago; this year it is again peppered liberally throughout. He chooses to work in his, "Gee, I wonder if this will stick" medium and the Hamilton King Award winning piece is typical, vintage Chris. The title, "The Stupid Club," was supplied by the client, *Esquire* magazine. Chris took on the job not only because he liked the subject matter, but because there are a handful of art directors that he simply enjoys working with and Amid Capici is one of them. Chris told me that the deadline for *Esquire* was about three weeks but that by the time the pencil sketches were okayed and other commissions had been moved off the board, he was looking at about five days to do the finish. Plenty of time!

The job was one that illustrators all hope will come their way, but one which is incredibly rare—a double-page illustration which has to stand by itself, unaided by text. The content was left to Chris's discretion and the only major change the magazine asked for was the hooded figure of Death which, up to the last moment, had been Karen Carpenter. I remember Chris discussing the job at the time. He had decided to place the dead celebrities in the barroom from "The Shining," but he knew that the story would have to be conveyed through facial expressions. For example, John Belushi, one of the oldest club members, looks quite comfortable with his surroundings. On the other hand, the newest member, Kurt Cobain, appears a little stunned at his inclusion.

Our telephone conversations keep me fully abreast of Chris's life, both at the drawing board and away from it. Of his many accomplishments he is by far the most proud of his family: Paula, his wife, and their sons, Trevor and Evan. But if you are able to get Chris off the subject of Trevor's batting average and onto illustration, you will be treated to a whirlwind of insight and information, whether it concerns the past, present, or future.

When I call Chris, I view the telephone lines as a massive set of jumper cables. Within minutes, my energy level is restored and work once again becomes play. I mention this as a lead-in to one last story and one which I feel exemplifies Chris the illustrator, both seen and unseen.

Somewhere here in *Illustrators 37* is a piece I did for a recent edition of *Moby Dick*. From day one, Chris was on the telephone wanting to know how it was going, how was I going to handle this scene, have I got a copy of the John Huston film?—on and on for over a year. I had delayed doing any of the drawings of the character Queequeg until the last minute. I knew that these drawings would be some of the most important in the book, but I could not locate an appropriate model.

"What type of drawings are you planning?" Chris finally asked and I faxed three two-inch square sketches. A week later, I received a FedEx package of reference photos Chris had taken of his friend Steve. The lighting was meticulous, as were the costuming and the props. Rarely had I ever worked from better material.

When discussing illustration, Chris doesn't dwell on the negative. I have never heard him complain about a deadline, an art director, or even a fee structure. His sole question is usually about how he can become better at his own job and sometimes, if he can, to help you become better at yours. This is what I mean when I refer to the unseen Chris. Whether it is through his teaching or his friendship, he has left his fingerprints on countless pages of this book.

Chris understands that his greatest strength is his desire to improve, for, as Da Vinci once wrote, "Stagnant water loses its purity." That is why the C.F. Payne you see in this volume is not the one represented a decade ago. It also means that the C.F. Payne of the next decade will not be the same as today's. Not necessarily better. Different.

Mark Summers

SPECIAL AWARDS 1995

1995 Dean Cornwell Recognition Award
Roy LaGrone

The members of the Society of Illustrators are fortunate to have counted Roy among our own for 32 years, until his untimely death in December 1993. In addition to his many contributions to the Society, he added a wonderful perspective to everything he touched.

Roy was a World War II pilot, one of the famous black Tuskegee Airmen, and subsequently a civilian career graphic designer, illustrator, art director, graphic coordinator, and artist.

Roy and I shared our love of aviation and involvement with the Society's Air Force Art Program. He was very active in the program, not only by documenting Air Force mission in the continental United States, but also through such activities as the TEAM SPIRIT exercises in Korea and the delivery of food and medicine to locations in the dissolving Soviet Union.

Much of Roy's Air Force art tells the stories of the sacrifices and contributions of his fellow Tuskegee Airmen and subsequent black United States Air Force pilots. Roy donated 24 of his paintings to the Air Force Art Collection in Washington, D.C.

He was long a member of the Society's Air Force Art Committee and served a term as its chairman. As a valued member of the committee of past Air Force Art Chairmen, he juried the Society's Air Force contributions, and he will be missed.

In general, Society members know their fellow members for their contributions of time and effort to its programs rather than from the details of their busy careers. As for Roy, he was a student at Pratt Institute in Brooklyn, New York; Tuskegee Institute in Alabama; and the University of Florence in Italy. His 44-year art career began in 1949 when he designed and illustrated book jackets for major New York publishers such as Harper and Row, Charles Scribner's Sons, Random House, and the Macmillan Company.

He served as illustrator and designer for *Family Circle Magazine* and *America*, the full-color Russian language picture magazine distributed in the Soviet Union by the U.S. Department of State. He also applied his talents as art director for Avon Books, *Pageant Magazine*, and the Columbia Broadcast System.

Roy ended his career as Art Director and Graphic Coordinator for the Medical Arts Section of the Rutgers Medical School in New Jersey.

His greatest artistic strengths lay in his strong sense of design and his belief in the importance of powerful drawing. He insisted on good drawing and practiced what he preached. With this award, the Society expresses its appreciation for Roy LaGrone's many contributions over the years. His wisdom, cheerfulness, humor, and infectious optimism will be long remembered.

Keith Ferris

1995 Arthur William Brown Achievement Award
Don Hall / *Hallmark Cards, Inc.*

To be a staff artist at Hallmark Cards in Kansas City, Missouri, is to be a pampered professional. The finest supplies are at your disposal; every new technology is at the end of your mouse; you have the camaraderie of hundreds of fellow artists; and you have the leading professional designers and artists brought to your doorstep to lecture and demonstrate.

To be an art student these days is to be a terrified unknown. Supplies are expensive and the checklist for them is long. What college can afford the very latest hardware and software? Students are as concerned about job opportunities as they are about assignment critiques. But over the past 15 years, with the thoughtful and generous support of Hallmark Cards, some of these anxieties have been eased for quite a few very talented young artists.

In 1980, the Society's Student Scholarship Competition published its first catalogue. It featured future stars: Peter deSève, Matt Mahurin, Mark Frederickson, John Ennis, Robert Hunt, John Jude Palencar, Hiro Kimura, and Judy Pedersen. Not too shabby.

It was with this ammunition that the Society in 1981 invited Hallmark Cards to join us in the recognition and support of the top college-level illustration students. Their sponsorship of the logistical expenses of the catalogue and program have allowed the Society's own fund raising to go directly to the students. That level is now $32,000 annually and growing. And the Hallmark Corporate Foundation Matching Grants have supported the illustration departments of the schools.

Over the years there has been both a consistent flow of excellent young artists at the over-100 schools nationwide that enter each year, and a consistent recognition of the program's unique opportunity by the top management at Hallmark—namely, Don Hall, son of the founder and Chairman of the Board.

During the early years, Hallmark's George Parker worked with the Society's John Witt. Then Garry Glissmeyer, now at Currants in Colorado, was an enthusiastic backer. And today, through the Foundation and its Vice President, Jeanne Bates, and her staff, the annual discussions are frank and very productive.

But Don Hall, whom the Society honored with its Gold Medal a few years ago has come to know the Society as a special place and this program as one worth supporting.

The dollar amounts have been generous by any not-for-profit organization's standards and the names of the students now professionals, are a who's who.

Recognizing the need for art education, both undergraduate through the Society's program and post-graduate to its own large staff, is a Hallmark hallmark. Artists in residence at Kansas City, like Tom Allen, John Collier, and Mark English, would echo that.

This award honors that multilevel achievement in art education.

Terrence Brown
Director, Society of Illustrators

CHAIRMAN'S MESSAGE

I must confess that I'm biased. I love representational, figurative, and still life painting, which I have always associated with illustration.

The most exciting experience for this chairman is to see pigmentation moved around on a flat surface until it becomes something emotional and psychological, and in terms of the physical, tactile. People who can observe, draw, and paint well are to be treasured.

Despite the present climate, I trust we are not a "dying breed," but the skies are overcast. To some extent, we as illustrators mirror the gallery world, and as I've noticed the decline in drawing skills there, so have I also noticed this in illustration. As we are no longer in a well-heeled Madison Avenue world, speed and small budgets give birth to small illustration, so for some the answer is the computer. We know technology is all around us, but I would argue that to segue into computerism neglects one of the artist's most fundamental building blocks—the ability to draw.

I would also mention that we are introducing an International section this year which I am sure will grow as word gets around.

Just a personal note! As a young artist in London, I always looked to America and feel very privileged to chair this year's Annual. From my first inclusion in the show in 1967, when I met many of the artists I had admired and who had stimulated me, it has been a tradition which I am proud to be a part of.

And, I thank all the lovely people who made this possible, including my Mum who sent me to drawing classes at age eleven.

WILSON MCLEAN

Wilson McLean
Chairman, 37th Annual Exhibition

Portrait by Daniel Schwartz

EDITORIAL JURY

CHARLES SANTORE
CHAIRMAN
Illustrator

HARVEY DINNERSTEIN
Artist/Instructor,
Art Students League

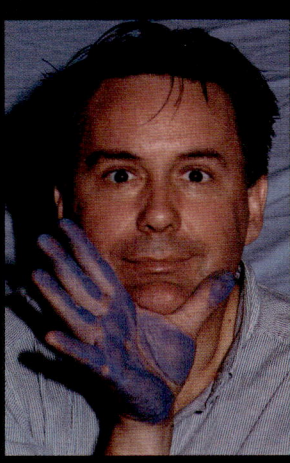

ANDRZEJ DUDZINSKI
Illustrator

EDITORIAL

AWARD WINNERS

JOHN COLLIER
Gold Medal

HANOCH PIVEN
Gold Medal

JACK ENDEWELT
Silver Medal

GREGORY MANCHESS
Silver Medal

RAFAL OLBINSKI
Silver Medal

KENT WILLIAMS
Silver Medal

1

Artist: **JOHN COLLIER**

Art Director: D. J. Stout

Client: Texas Monthly

Medium: Pastel, gouache on watercolor paper

Size: 23" x 30"

Editorial Gold Medal
JOHN COLLIER

This assignment for *Texas Monthly* was to illustrate a piece on native Texas animals. This is the coyote, which, according to John Collier, was "the guiltiest looking fellow you ever saw." Collier and Art Director D.J. Stout had settled on headlights to illuminate the beast.
But when John came upon this Dallas setting—with a street light glowing on a cedar—it was too good to pass up.

Artist: **HANOCH PIVEN**

Art Directors: Richard Baker
Lisa Wagner

Client: US magazine

Medium: Gouache and microphone

Editorial Gold Medal
HANOCH PIVEN

Born in Montevideo, Uruguay, in 1963, Piven was raised in Israel from age eleven. He came to New York and graduated from the School of Visual Arts in 1992 and has been working and receiving awards ever since. "I have been drawing caricatures all my life. When getting a likeness was not a challenge any more, I became cocky and said to myself, O.K., let's see if you can get a likeness without drawing the eyes. O.K., now no eyes and no mouth…etc. Having set myself up that way I feel as if I'm 'cheating' when I include too many features in a caricature. I feel very lucky that at this early point in my career I have been able to discover a personal direction which I feel is honest and unique."

3

Artist: **JACK ENDEWELT**

Medium: Oil on board

Size: 9" x 12"

Editorial Silver Medal
JACK ENDEWELT

"My fascination with airplanes occurred at the same time as my obsession with making pictures did. I was about five years old when World War II broke out and my formative years were filled with images of planes and other war machines and the people who operated them. I have read that cave painters used animals as their subject matter, in part to identify with their strength and beauty. I suppose I did the same with airplanes when I was a boy. I've always thought that even the most ungainly of that era's aircraft had a beauty. My early fascination with making pictures became my chosen career, and after my education at the School of Visual Arts, I became an illustrator. Many years later I find myself teaching, administrating, and still making pictures. The little boy is still there too, and he's still fascinated."

4

Artist: **GREGORY MANCHESS**

Art Director: Dwayne J. Flinchum

Client: Omni

Medium: Oil on board

Size: 25 ½" x 18"

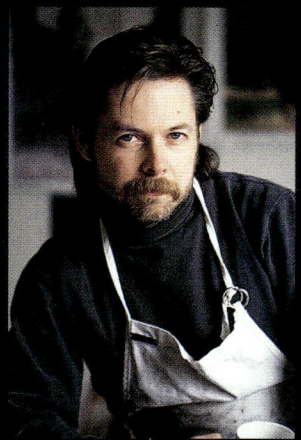

Editorial Silver Medal
GREGORY MANCHESS

"No artist is ever free of his influences. But that's the good news. Question is, how to utilize those influences and come out with ourselves. For this piece I embraced my favorite artists of the late 1800s to visualize an early feminist of science and flight, a female Jules Verne working with wood and wire. I'm drawn to mythic imagery and archetypes and how they relate to all of us. Great thing about Dwayne's art direction is that he's aware of letting an artist express his interests."

5

Artist: **RAFAL OLBINSKI**

Art Director: Cathryn Mezzo

Client: Omni

Medium: Acrylic on canvas

Size: 30" x 20"

Editorial Silver Medal
RAFAL OLBINSKI

"I owe this medal to the good taste and sensitivity of Cathy Mezzo who chose the painting from the exhibition of my work at the Nahan Gallery in Soho and used it for a pictorial article in Omni magazine. This painting is of particular personal meaning for me because I dedicated it to my daughter Natalia for her sixth birthday."

Artist: **KENT WILLIAMS**

Art Director: Roy Comiskey

Client: Security Management Magazine

Medium: Oil on styrene

Size: 20" x 24"

Editorial Silver Medal
KENT WILLIAMS

"Can you pick the cup that the pea is under? The pooch sure can. This painting was for an article entitled "The Canine Connection" and dealt with the use of dogs for drug detection in the work place. A lighthearted one for me, this illustration stars my own scoundrel, Mayse."

7
Artist: **SKIP LIEPKE**
Art Director: Steve Connaster
Client: Private Clubs
Medium: Oil on canvas
Size: 18" x 22"

8
Artist: **MARSHALL ARISMAN**
Art Director: Christina Hansen
Client: Alaska Magazine
Medium: Oil on ragboard
Size: 22 1/2" x 25"

9
Artist: **MIKE BENNY**
Art Directors: Tom Staebler
Kerig Pope
Client: Playboy
Medium: Acrylic on board
Size: 18"x 18"

8

9

10
Artist: **PHILIP BURKE**
Art Director: Kerry Tremain
Client: Mother Jones Magazine
Medium: Oil on canvas
Size: 48" x 36"

11
Artist: **MARSHALL ARISMAN**
Art Director: Cathryn Mezzo
Client: Omni
Medium: Oil on ragboard
Size: 21 1/2" x 16 1/2"

12
Artist: **KELYNN ALDER**
Art Director: Christine Curry
Client: The New Yorker
Medium: Oil on paper
Size: 8" x 11 1/2"

13
Artist: **BILL JAMES**
Medium: Pastel on cardboard
Size: 23 1/2" x 33"

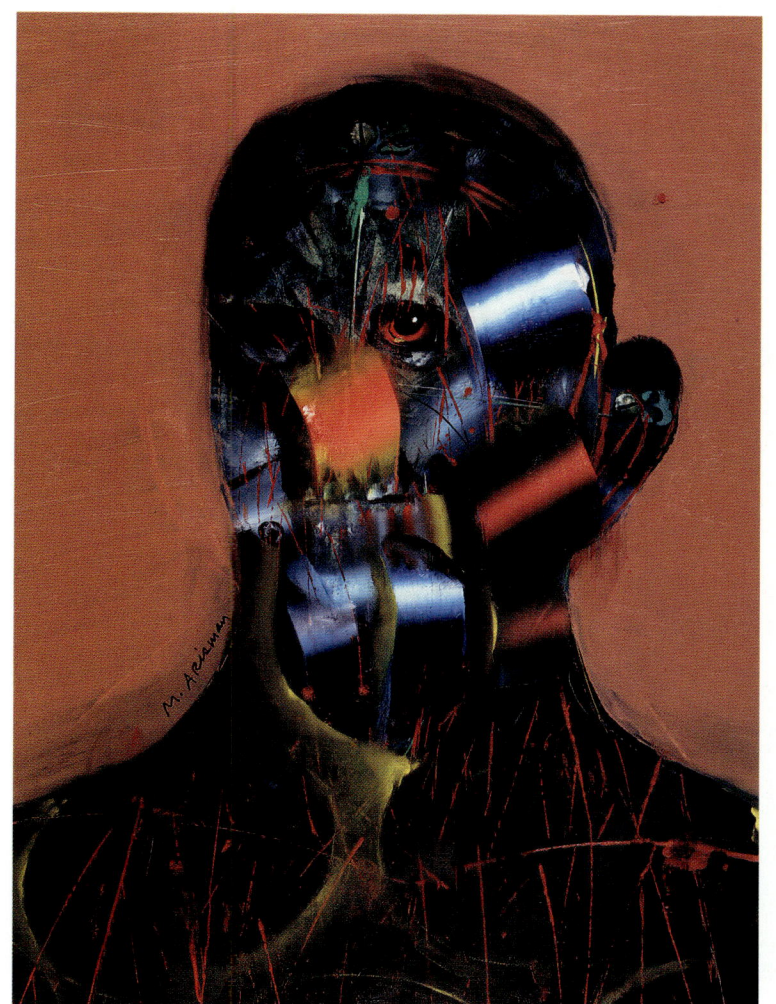

11

12

13

14
Artist: **GUY BILLOUT**
Art Director: Christian Kuypers
Client: Time
Medium: Watercolor, airbrush on paper
Size: 9" x 6 1/2"

15
Artist: **N. ASCENCIOS**
Art Director: Christine Curry
Client: The New Yorker
Medium: Oil on canvas
Size: 28 1/2" x 37"

16
Artist: **DENNIS BALOGH**
Art Director: Dennis Balogh
Client: Beacon Magazine
Medium: Charcoal pencil, watercolor on Arches
Size: 16" x 12 1/2"

17
Artist: **DON ASMUSSEN**
Art Director: Diana Shantick
Client: The Los Angeles Times
Medium: Pen & ink, collage on board
Size: 13 1/2" x 8 1/2"

18
Artist: **BRALDT BRALDS**
Art Director: D. J. Stout
Client: Texas Monthly
Medium: Oil on masonite
Size: 19" x 19"

19
Artist: **RAUL COLON**
Art Director: Julia Kushnirsky
Client: Warner Books
Medium: Mixed

20
Artist: **PHILIP BURKE**
Art Director: Fred Woodward
Client: Rolling Stone
Medium: Oil on canvas

21
Artist: **JOSEPH SALINA**
Art Directors: Arthur Hochstein
Kenneth Smith
Client: Time
Medium: Acrylic on board

22
Artist: **PHILIP BURKE**
Art Director: Fred Woodward
Client: Rolling Stone
Medium: Oil on canvas

18

19

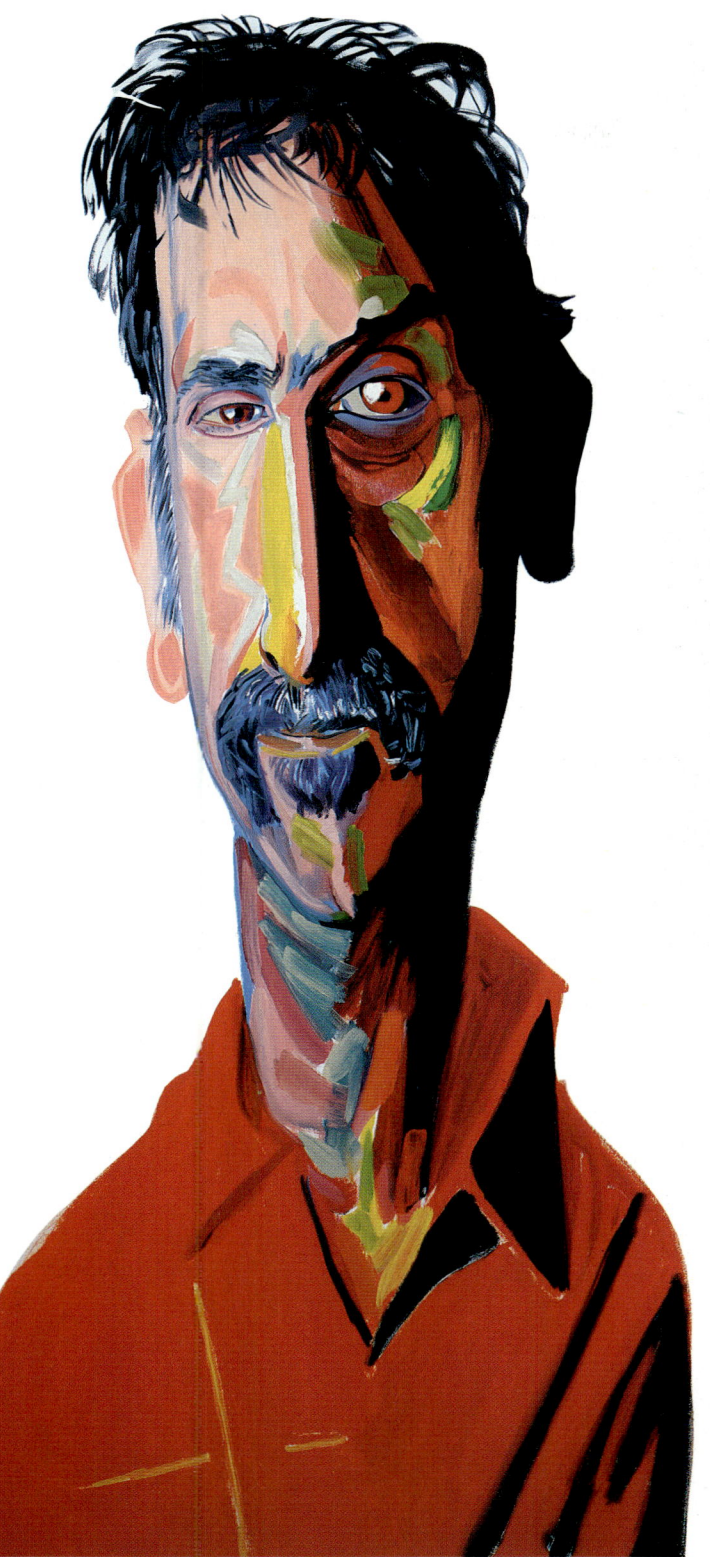
20

21

22

23
Artist: **BARRY BLITT**
Art Director: Margot Frankel
Client: Town & Country
Medium: Watercolor
Size: 9 1/2" x 8"

24
Artist: **THOMAS BENNETT**
Medium: Monotype on paper
Size: 19" x 13"

25
Artist: **MARK SUMMERS**
Art Director: Steve Heller
Client: The New York Times Magazine
Medium: Scratchboard
Size: 6" x 9"

26
Artist: **R.O. BLECHMAN**
Art Director: Christine Curry
Client: The New Yorker
Medium: Watercolor, collage on paper
Size: 12" x 9"

27
Artist: **W. B. PARK**
Medium: Oil on canvas
Size: 36" x 36"

24

25

Henry James

26

27

28
Artist: **KINUKO CRAFT**
Art Director: Ina Salz
Client: Worth Magazine
Medium: Mixed

29
Artist: **JOE CIARDIELLO**
Art Director: Alice Degenhardt
Client: Creative Living
Medium: Pen, watercolor, collage on paper
Size: 17" x 12 1/2"

30
Artist: **JOE CIARDIELLO**
Art Director: Joseph P. Connolly
Client: Boys' Life
Medium: Pen, watercolor on paper
Size: 13" x 9"

31
Artist: **WILLIAM BRAMHALL**
Art Director: Jim Condon
Client: The Wall Street Journal
Medium: Pen & ink
Size: 11" x 14"

32
Artist: **TOM CURRY**
Art Director: J. Porter
Client: Yankee Magazine
Medium: Acrylic on board
Size: 13 1/2" x 12 1/2"

33
Artist: **TOM CURRY**
Art Director: Tricia McGinty
Client: New Woman
Medium: Acrylic on board
Size: 16" x 12"

34
Artist: **TOM CURRY**
Art Director: Alisann Marshall
Client: American Way
Medium: Acrylic on board
Size: 16 1/2" x 12"

35
Artist: **BOB A. DAVIS**
Medium: Gouache on board
Size: 14 1/2" x 27 1/2"

32

33

34

35

36
Artist: **PETER de SÈVE**
Art Director: Tina Klem
Client: Four Seasons Hotels & Resorts Magazine
Medium: Watercolor, ink on paper
Size: 11" x 8"

37
Artist: **PETER de SÈVE**
Art Director: Francoise Mouly
Client: The New Yorker
Medium: Watercolor, ink on paper

38
Artist: **PETER de SÈVE**
Art Director: John Korpics
Client: Premiere
Medium: Watercolor, ink on paper

39
Artist: **JEFF DODSON**
Art Director: D. J. Stout
Client: Texas Monthly
Medium: Mixed on paper
Size: 20" x 16"

40
Artist: **RICHARD DOWNS**
Art Director: Martha Geering
Client: Sierra
Medium: Monotype on paper
Size: 19 1/2" x 14 1/2"

37

38

39

40

41
Artist: **TRISTAN ELWELL**
Art Director: Paul Richer
Client: Sesame Street Magazine
Medium: Oil on board
Size: 11" x 8 1/2"

42
Artist: **BLAIR DRAWSON**
Art Director: Richard Baker
Client: US magazine
Medium: Mixed
Size: 15" x 11 1/2"

43
Artist: **PHIL BOATWRIGHT**
Art Director: Spencer Grahl
Client: Moody Magazine
Medium: Oil, acrylic on Strathmore board
Size: 17 1/2" x 14 1/2"

44
Artist: **MARSHALL ARISMAN**
Art Director: Dwayne Flinchum
Client: Penthouse
Medium: Oil on ragboard
Size: 22 1/2" x 28 1/2"

41

42

43

44

45

Artist: **ALAN E. COBER**

Art Directors: Fred Woodward
Gail Anderson

Client: Rolling Stone

Medium: Ink, watercolor, Prismacolor on Arches paper

Size: 12 ½" x 9"

46

Artist: **BART FORBES**

Art Director: Joseph P. Connolly

Client: Boys' Life

Medium: Oil on canvas

Size: 19" x 19"

47

Artist: **JOHN FERRY**

Art Director: Tom Staebler

Client: Playboy

Medium: Oil on masonite

Size: 11" x 11"

48

Artist: **JOHN FERRY**

Art Director: Kevin Swanson

Client: Kansas City Magazine

Medium: Acrylic on masonite

Size: 5" x 5"

46

47

48

49

Artist: **PAUL ANDERSON**
Art Director: Beverly Blake
Client: Wireless Design & Development
Medium: Oil on canvas
Size: 9 1/2" x 9"

50

Artist: **ALLEN GARNS**
Art Director: Don Lambson
Client: WordPerfect Magazine
Medium: Pastel on paper
Size: 18" x 16"

51

Artist: **JACK N. UNRUH**
Art Director: Albert Chiang
Client: Islands
Medium: Ink, watercolor on Strathmore
Size: 15" x 18"

52

Artist: **JOHN COLLIER**
Art Director: Janet Froelich
Client: The New York Times Magazine
Medium: Pastel on paper
Size: 19" x 22 1/2"

49

50

EDITORIAL
Illustrators 37

51

52

53
Artist: **MARK FREDRICKSON**
Art Directors: Arthur Hochstein
Kenneth Smith
Client: Time
Medium: Mixed
Size: 10 1/2" x 9"

54
Artist: **SCOTT SWALES**
Art Director: Nancy Duckworth
Client: Los Angeles Times Magazine
Medium: Pastel, acrylic on paper
Size: 14" x 11 1/8"

55
Artist: **ROBERT RISKO**
Art Director: Fred Woodward
Client: Rolling Stone
Medium: Gouache

56
Artist: **JOHN H. HOWARD**
Art Directors: Judy Garlan
Robin Gilmore-Barnes
Client: The Atlantic Monthly
Medium: Acrylic on canvas
Size: 23 1/2" x 17 1/2"

57
Artist: **JOSEPH DANIEL FIEDLER**
Art Director: Daniel Pfeffer
Client: Lears
Medium: Alkyd on paper
Size: 14" x 11"

53

54

55

56

57

58
Artist: **BRAD HOLLAND**
Art Director: Dwayne Flinchum
Client: Penthouse
Medium: Acrylic
Size: 14 1/2" x 19"

59
Artist: **CYNTHIA J. CARMICHAEL**
Art Director: Lewis Calver
Client: Pulse Magazine
Medium: Cell paint, airbrush, herculine over photo
Size: 16 1/2" x 13 1/2"

60
Artist: **SKIP LIEPKE**
Art Director: Fred Woodward
Client: Rolling Stone
Medium: Watercolor on board
Size: 9 1/2" x 14 1/2"

61
Artist: **BILL JAMES**
Medium: Pastel on Canson Mi-Teintes paper
Size: 26" x 32"

58

59

60

61

62
Artist: **DAVID GROVE**
Art Director: Mike Christensen
Client: Covey Leadership Center
Medium: Gouache, acrylic on board
Size: 13" x 14 1/2"

63
Artist: **TERRY ALLEN**
Art Director: Mira Ramji-Stein
Client: OEM Magazine
Medium: Airbrush on board
Size: 16" x 14"

64
Artist: **DAVID JOHNSON**
Art Directors: Nicholas D. Torello
Joy Makon
Client: Scholastic Inc.
Medium: Mixed
Size: 15" x 22"

65
Artist: **JORDIN ISIP**
Art Director: Judy Garlan
Client: The Atlantic Monthly
Medium: Mixed on paper
Size: 24" x 18 1/2"

66
Artist: **TIM HUSSEY**
Art Director: Richard Baker
Client: US magazine
Medium: Mixed on paper
Size: 14 1/2" X 11 1/2"

62

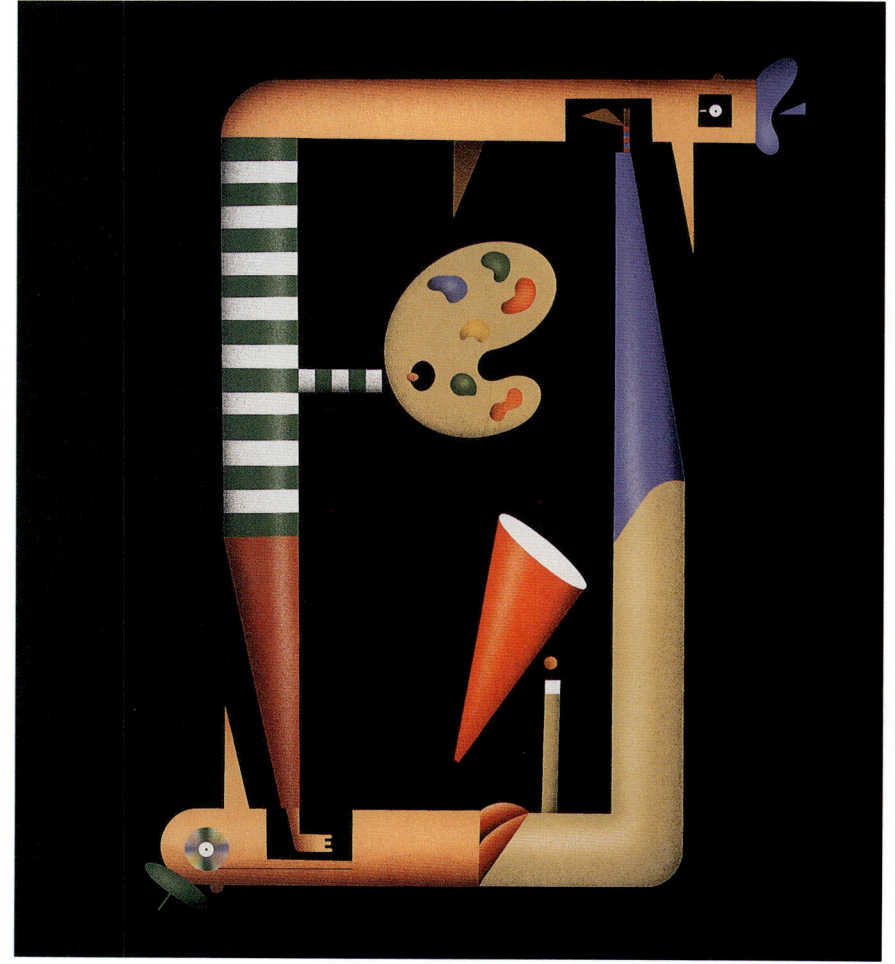
63

64

65

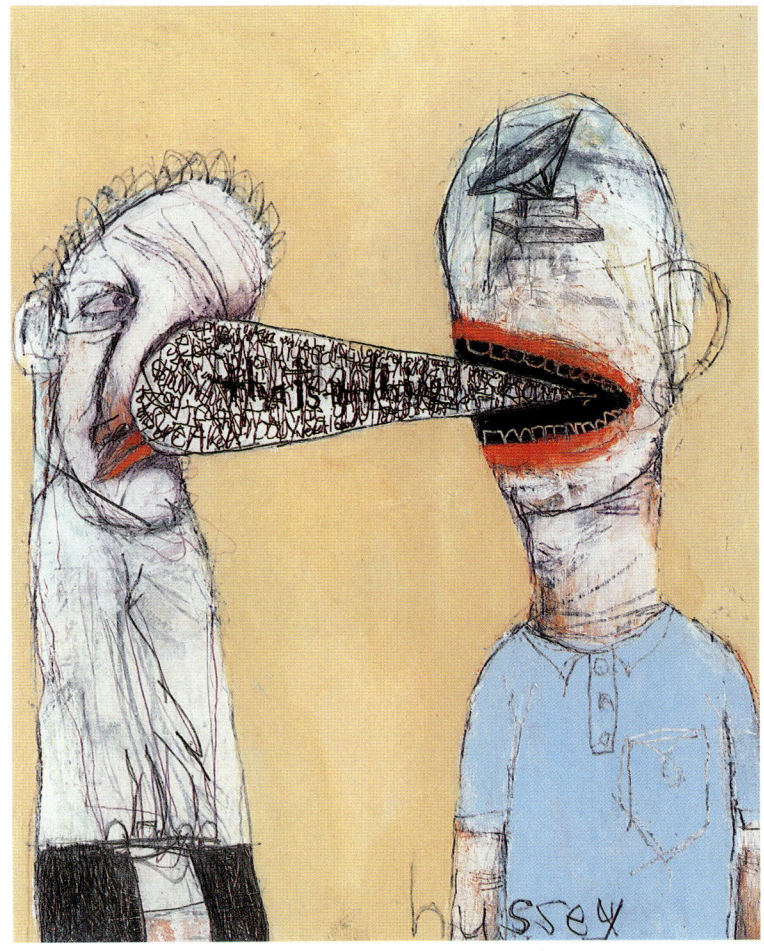
66

67

Artist: **ANITA KUNZ**

Art Director: Cathryn Mezzo

Client: Omni

Medium: Watercolor, gouache on board

Size: 12" x 8 1/2"

68

Artist: **MATT MAHURIN**

Art Director: Fred Woodward

Client: Rolling Stone

Medium: Mixed

Size: 9" X 8"

69

Artist: **JAMES KIMAK**

Art Director: James Kimak

Client: Prodigy

Medium: Pastel, wash on board. Optimized for online use through Photoshop

Size: 8" x 12"

70

Artist: **ROBERT GOLDSTROM**

Art Director: Judy Garlan

Client: The Atlantic Monthly

Medium: Oil on canvas

Size: 8 1/2" x 15"

68

69

70

71
Artist: **GARY KELLEY**
Art Director: Judy Garlan
Client: The Atlantic Monthly
Medium: Pastel on paper
Size: 17 1/2" x 21 1/2"

72
Artist: **N. ASCENCIOS**
Art Directors: Arthur Hochstein
Kenneth Smith
Client: Time
Medium: Oil on canvas
Size: 18" x 15"

73
Artist: **EDWARD GOREY**
Art Director: Ina Salz
Client: Worth Magazine
Medium: Mixed

74
Artist: **DANUTA JARECKA**
Art Director: Alma Phipps
Client: Chief Executive
Medium: Gouache on paper
Size: 12" x 9 1/2"

75
Artists: **MARA KURTZ**
SASHA KURTZ
Art Directors: Carl Lehmann-Haupt
Nancy Cohen
Client: Metropolis
Medium: Polaroid transfer,
watercolor on paper
Size: 3 1/2" x 4"

71

72

73

74

75

76

Artist: **SKIP LIEPKE**

Art Director: Gary Kelley

Client: The North American Review

Medium: Oil on canvas

Size: 22" x 16"

77

Artist: **BRAD HOLLAND**

Art Director: Dwayne Flinchum

Client: Penthouse

Medium: Acrylic

Size: 14 1/2" X 19"

78

Artist: **SKIP LIEPKE**

Art Directors: Mike Diiola
David Cuccurito

Client: Penthouse

Medium: Oil on canvas

Size: 20" x 18"

79

Artist: **LUBA LUKOVA**

Art Director: Lisa Kocaurek

Client: Ms.

Medium: Gouache on board

Size: 16" x 8"

EDITORIAL
Illustrators 37

77

78

79

80

Artist: **GARY KELLEY**

Art Director: Lisa Wrigley

Client: Rocky Mountain Magazine

Medium: Pastel on paper

Size: 20 1/2" x 15 1/2"

81

Artist: **BRAD HOLLAND**

Art Director: D. J. Stout

Client: Texas Monthly

Medium: Acrylic on Masonite

Size: 18 1/2" x 25 1/2"

82

Artist: **MATT MAHURIN**

Client: Spin

Medium: Mixed

Size: 19 1/2" X 15 1/2"

83

Artist: **STEPHEN T. JOHNSON**

Art Director: Christine Curry

Client: The New Yorker

Medium: Pastel, watercolor on paper

Size: 29" x 17"

80

81

82

83

84
Artist: **TERESA FASOLINO**
Art Director: Bob Mansfield
Client: Forbes
Medium: Acrylic on canvas
Size: 18 1/2" x 14 1/2"

85
Artist: **WILSON McLEAN**
Art Director: Kerig Pope
Client: Playboy
Medium: Oil on canvas
Size: 18 1/2" x 35 1/2"

86
Artist: **JOSÉ ORTEGA**
Art Director: Jessica Helfand
Client: Philadelphia Inquirer
Medium: Mixed
Size: 11" x 9"

87
Artist: **WILSON McLEAN**
Medium: Oil on canvas
Size: 17 1/2" x 17 1/2"

84

EDITORIAL
Illustrators 37

85

86

87

88

Artist: **HENRIK DRESCHER**

Art Directors: Arthur Hochstein
Kenneth Smith

Client: Time

Medium: Collage

Size: 8" x 6 1/2"

89

Artist: **WILSON McLEAN**

Art Director: Dwayne Flinchum

Client: Penthouse

Medium: Oil on canvas

Size: 19 1/2" x 24"

90

Artist: **FRANCIS LIVINGSTON**

Art Director: Sara Hollander

Client: Mortgage Banking

Medium: Oil on board

Size: 23" x 17"

91

Artist: **JOEL PETER JOHNSON**

Art Director: Rose Galiloto

Client: Forecast

Medium: Oil, acrylic on board

Size: 8" x 6"

EDITORIAL
Illustrators 37

89

90

91

92
Artist: **PAUL DAVIS**
Art Director: Arthur Hochstein
Client: Time
Medium: Acrylic on board
Size: 15" x 11"

93
Artist: **MICHAEL PARASKEVAS**
Art Director: Kelly Doe
Client: The Washington Post Magazine
Medium: Acrylic on paper
Size: 35" x 28"

94
Artist: **CHRIS GALL**
Art Director: Julia Kushnirsky
Client: Warner Books
Medium: Mixed

95
Artist: **MICHAEL PARASKEVAS**
Art Director: Judy Garlan
Client: The Atlantic Monthly
Medium: Acrylic on paper
Size: 20" x 30"

EDITORIAL
Illustrators 37

93

94

95

96
Artist: **JOHN COLLIER**
Art Director: Fred Woodward
Client: Rolling Stone
Medium: Pastel

97
Artist: **HANOCH PIVEN**
Art Director: Judy Garlan
Client: The Atlantic Monthly
Medium: Mixed on paper
Size: 9" x 6"

98
Artist: **ROBERT ANDREW PARKER**
Art Director: Christine Curry
Client: The New Yorker
Medium: Monoprint, watercolor

99
Artist: **ROBERT ANDREW PARKER**
Art Director: Christine Curry
Client: The New Yorker
Medium: Mixed

97

98

99

100

Artist: **PHIL BOATWRIGHT**

Art Director: Laurie Shattuck

Client: Virtue Magazine

Medium: Mixed, assemblage on Strathmore board

Size: 16" x 12"

101

Artist: **C. F. PAYNE**

Art Director: Amid Capici

Client: Esquire

Medium: Mixed on board

Size: 16" x 23"

102

Artist: **C. F. PAYNE**

Art Director: Arthur Hochstein

Client: Time

Medium: Mixed

Size: 14" x 11"

103

Artist: **C. F. PAYNE**

Art Director: Kelly Doe

Client: The Washington Post Magazine

Medium: Mixed on board

Size: 12" x 15"

100

101

102

103

104

Artist: **THEO RUDNAK**

Art Director: Judy Garlan

Client: The Atlantic Monthly

Medium: Gouache on cotton Strathmore

Size: 18" x 18"

105

Artist: **THEO RUDNAK**

Art Director: Sandy Rumreich

Client: Federal Express

Medium: Gouache on cotton Strathmore

Size: 20" x 16"

106

Artist: **WILLIAM LOW**

Art Director: Sharon Nelson

Client: Milwaukee Magazine

Medium: Oil on board

Size: 14" x 16 1/2"

107

Artist: **JOHN SPRINGS**

Art Director: Richard Baker

Client: US magazine

Medium: Ink, acrylic on glazed paper

104

105

106

107

108

Artist: **DOUG STEVENS**

Art Directors: Joe Scopin
John Kascht

Client: The Washington Times

Medium: Computer generated

Size: 10 1/2" x 6 3/4"

109

Artist: **JOSEPH H. SULKOWSKI**

Art Director: Mindy Phelps Stanton

Client: Field & Stream

Medium: Oil on canvas

Size: 24" x 36"

110

Artist: **RICK SEALOCK**

Art Director: Jef Capaldi

Client: American Medical News

Medium: Mixed

Size: 15 1/4" x 11 1/2"

111

Artist: **RICK SEALOCK**

Art Director: Nancy Duckworth

Client: Los Angeles Times Magazine

Medium: Mixed

Size: 15 1/2" x 12 1/2"

109

110

111

112

Artist: **DUGALD STERMER**

Art Director: Matthew Drace

Client: Travel & Leisure

Medium: Pencil, watercolor on Arches

Size: 20" x 14"

113

Artist: **BURT SILVERMAN**

Art Director: Kenneth Smith

Client: Time

Medium: Oil on paper

Size: 14 1/2" x 10"

114

Artist: **TULLIO PERICOLI**

Art Director: Christine Curry

Client: The New Yorker

Medium: Mixed

115

Artist: **PETER SIS**

Art Director: Charles Hess

Client: USC Health & Medicine

Medium: Watercolor

Size: 20" x 12"

116

Artist: **AGATHA SOHN**

Art Directors: Fo Wilson
Anissa Smith

Client: HealthQuest

Medium: Oil on photo paper

Size: 11" x 17"

113

114

115

116

117

Artist: **GREG SPALENKA**
Art Director: Mary Multhauf
Client: Milwaukee Magazine
Medium: Mixed
Size: 12" x 9"

118

Artist: **ELWOOD H. SMITH**
Art Director: Mare Early
Client: Chicago Tribune Magazine
Medium: Watercolor, ink on paper
Size: 14" x 12"

119

Artist: **GREG SPALENKA**
Art Director: Tricia McGinty
Client: New Woman
Medium: Mixed
Size: 12" x 9"

120

Artist: **KENT WILLIAMS**
Art Director: Dwayne Flinchum
Client: Penthouse
Medium: Oil on panel
Size: 24" x 24"

118

119

120

121
Artist: **BILL MAYER**
Art Director: Lauren Levi
Client: Texas Realtor
Medium: Airbrush on board
Size: 16" x 15"

122
Artist: **ARNOLD ROTH**
Art Director: John Tan
Client: Field & Stream
Medium: Watercolor
Size: 2' x 3'

123
Artist: **KENT WILLIAMS**
Art Director: Cathryn Mezzo
Client: Omni
Medium: Oil on canvas
Size: 18" x 24"

124
Artist: **DAVID TILLINGHAST**
Art Director: David Tillinghast
Client: Gail Imstepf
Medium: Acrylic on canvas
Size: 14" x 12"

121

122

123

124

125

Artist: **SANDRA HENDLER**

Art Director: D. J. Stout

Client: Texas Monthly

Medium: Oil on canvas

Size: 9" x 12"

126

Artist: **TIM JESSELL**

Art Director: Cynthia Currie

Client: Kiplinger's Personal Finance Magazine

Medium: Mixed on paper

Size: 10 1/2" x 12 1/2"

127

Artist: **ROBERT ANDREW PARKER**

Art Director: Christine Curry

Client: The New Yorker

Medium: Monoprint, watercolor

128

Artist: **CALEF BROWN**

Art Director: Christine Curry

Client: The New Yorker

Medium: Oil, acrylic on board

129

Artist: **DUGALD STERMER**

Art Director: John Tan

Client: Field & Stream

Medium: Pencil, watercolor on Arches

Size: 20" x 14"

125

126

EDITORIAL
Illustrators 37

127

128

129

130

Artist: **JACK N. UNRUH**
Art Director: Tim Cain
Client: Kiplinger's Personal Finance Magazine
Medium: Ink, watercolor on board
Size: 17" x 14"

132

Artist: **GLYNIS SWEENY**
Art Director: George Mimnaugh
Client: Baltimore City Paper
Medium: Prismacolor
Size: 14" x 11"

133

Artist: **MARK RYDEN**
Art Director: Janet Waegle
Client: Time
Medium: Acrylic on board
Size: 8" x 16"

134

Artist: **DAVID SHANNON**
Art Director: Sheila Himmel
Client: West Magazine
Medium: Acrylic on board
Size: 14" x 12"

130

132

133

134

135
Artist: **ROBERT GOLDSTROM**
Art Director: Janet Froelich
Client: The New York Times
Medium: Oil on canvas
Size: 9" x 8"

136
Artist: **FRANCES JETTER**
Art Director: Patrick Flynn
Client: The Progressive
Medium: Linocut on paper
Size: 16 x 12"

137
Artist: **DAN SWEETMAN**
Art Director: Diana Shantic
Client: Los Angeles Times Calendar
Medium: Acrylic
Size: 12" x 12"

138
Artist: **ANDREA VENTURA**
Art Directors: Judy Garlan
　　　　　　　Robin Gilmore-Barnes
Client: The Atlantic Monthly
Medium: Acrylic, charcoal on paper

135

136

137

138

BOOK JURY

BRALDT BRALDS
CHAIRMAN
Illustrator

DAVID BAMFORD
Art Director, Putnam Berkley Publishing Group

BLAIR DRAWSON
Illustrator

LOUISE FILI
*Graphic Designer,
Louise Fili, Ltd.*

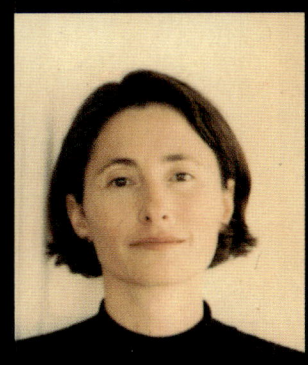
VIVIENNE FLESHER
Illustrator

HEIDE OBERHEIDE
Illustrator

D.J. STOUT
*Art Director,
Texas Monthly*

JACK N. UNRUH
Illustrator

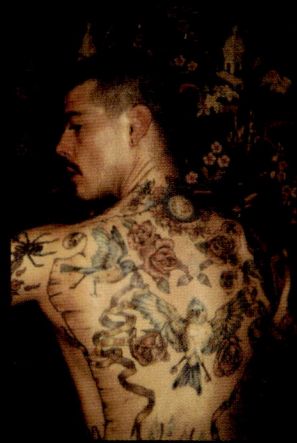
THOMAS WOODRUFF
Illustrator/Teacher/Curator

BOOK

AWARD WINNERS

MARK RYDEN
Gold Medal

GENNADY SPIRIN
Gold Medal

MARK SUMMERS
Gold Medal

DANIEL ADEL
Silver Medal

ANTHONY BROWNE
Silver Medal

RAUL COLON
Silver Medal

139

Artist: **MARK RYDEN**

Art Director: Craig Yo

Client: Mattel

Medium: Oil on board

Size: 24" x 36"

Book Gold Medal
MARK RYDEN

"Barbie doesn't naturally bend with contrapasto and palms out, so in order to pose her I tried to melt her in the microwave. She just turned to liquid and smelled up the kitchen. Fortunately, I quickly got another Barbie at a 24-hour Thrifty nearby (I work late at night). This time I boiled her. It worked great. The little girl is my niece Justine. She prefers dinosaurs to Barbie dolls but managed to pose with an adoring look."

Artist: **GENNADY SPIRIN**

Art Director: Atha Tehon

Client: Dial Books for Young Readers

Medium: Watercolor

Size: 12" x 19"

Book Gold Medal
GENNADY SPIRIN

Gennady Spirin, who trained at the Moscow Art Academies and emigrated to the United States three years ago, has received three consecutive Gold Medals from the Society's Annuals. His collaborations with Atha Tehon at Dial Books for Young Readers have also been highly recognized by other children's book award events. Spirin greatly appreciates the freedom Atha Tehon has given him to pursue his ideas.

Artist: **MARK SUMMERS**

Art Director: John Kelly

Client: Barnes & Noble

Medium: Scratchboard

Size: 8 ½" x 11"

Book Gold Medal
MARK SUMMERS

Mark Summers' first illustrated book for Barnes & Noble was Herman Melville's *Moby Dick*. It required 13 images, created over a year's time. He noted that there was a crunch at the end to complete the project, but he settled on treating each piece as a separate work with its own problems to solve. He drew heavily on his own sources for the concepts, including clippings, movies, and videos. Of course, Rockwell Kent and John Huston would seem to be influences, but Summers admits that they were too good to improve on and that he strove to supplement them. This image is the last in the book—all are about to meet their doom, so the whale's jaw portends their tombstones.

Artist: **DANIEL ADEL**
Art Director: Jeri Hansen
Client: Viking Penguin
Medium: Oil on board
Size: 8" x 8"

Book Silver Medal
DANIEL ADEL

"For the last several years I have been illustrating, painting portraits (academic portraits of academics, mostly), and doing pretentious still-lifes of industrial objects in excessively large Dutch-style frames. The chance to work with world-famous author/squash player Jon Scieska on *The Book That Jack Wrote* not only provided an exciting once-in-a-lifetime opportunity to re-connect with my inner child and get in touch with my feelings about rats, bugs, and over-dressed cats, but also was a chance to combine my illustration, portraiture, and interest in framing into one exciting tour de-France.

This particular piece was my first dental self-portrait and constitutes a sincere tribute to my parents' investment in years of painful orthodontia and is dedicated to my late cat Max (1963-1984)."

143

Artist: **ANTHONY BROWNE**

Art Director: Lynn Boulton

Client: Turner Publishing, Inc.

Medium: Mixed

Size: 10" x 7"

Book Silver Medal
ANTHONY BROWNE

"The process of writing and illustrating a picture book is like planning a film. The first thing I always do is make a storyboard, 32 rectangles filled with indecipherable scribbles that are neither pictures nor words.

"My fascination with gorillas is related to my father, a big man and a war hero who was also artistic and sensitive. It's the dual nature of Kong which attracts me—the terrifying beast who is in reality a gentle, beautiful creature. Memories of my father's death have terrible echoes of Kong's fall from the Empire State Building. So, although the story of a gigantic ape terrorizing the people of an island in the Indian Ocean might seem a long way from the experiences of a boy from the North of England, it's far more personal than it might appear."

144

Artist: **RAUL COLON**

Art Director: Denise Cronin

Client: Alfred A. Knopf

Medium: Watercolor, colored pencil on paper

Size: 14" x 16"

Book Silver Medal
RAUL COLON

Raul Colon is a native of New York who studied commercial art and spent ten years in an instructional television center in south Florida. He is a freelance illustrator whose work appears regularly in *Business Week*, *The New Yorker*, and *The New York Times*. He has received awards for excellence from the Florida Press Club and *Annual Report Five*, and a broadcast designer award for his poster of the "Shaka Zulu" TV mini-series. Influenced by Matt Mahurin, Brad Holland, Gary Kelley, and John Collier, he says, "I like very dark stuff. But I think every artist has to move on, change, push."

145
Artist: **WILLIAM JOYCE**
Art Director: Christine Kettner
Client: HarperCollins
Medium: Oil on Bristol board
Size: 13 1/2" x 27"

146
Artist: **WILLIAM JOYCE**
Art Director: Christine Kettner
Client: HarperCollins
Medium: Oil on Bristol board
Size: 15 1/8" x 20 1/8"

147
Artist: **LINDA BLECK**
Art Directors: Emily Hayes
Michael Bierut
Client: Mohawk Paper
Medium: Gouache on Strathmore Bristol
Size: 10" x 15"

148
Artist: **HENRIK DRESCHER**
Art Director: Henrik Drescher
Client: Harcourt Brace & Co.
Medium: Mixed

145

146

147

148

149

Artist: **RAUL COLON**
Art Director: Denise Cronin
Client: Alfred A. Knopf
Medium: Watercolor, colored pencil on paper
Size: 14 1/4" x 15 3/4"

150

Artist: **RAUL COLON**
Art Director: Denise Cronin
Client: Alfred A. Knopf
Medium: Watercolor, pencil on paper
Size: 14 1/4" x 15 3/4"

151

Artist: **MARK SUMMERS**
Art Director: John Kelly
Client: Barnes & Noble
Medium: Scratchboard
Size: 8 1/2" x 11"

152

Artist: **TERESA FASOLINO**
Art Director: Jackie Merri Meyer
Client: Warner Books
Medium: Acrylic on canvas
Size: 20 1/2" x 13 1/2"

149

150

151

152

153

Artist: **KINUKO CRAFT**

Art Director: Frank Metz

Client: Simon & Schuster

Medium: Oil, watercolor on board

Size: 17" x 14 1/2"

154

Artist: **ALAN E. COBER**

Art Director: Don Owens

Client: American Jury by Trial Foundation

Medium: Ink, watercolor on Arches cover

Size: 11" x 8"

155

Artist: **ETIENNE DELESSERT**

Art Director: Rita Marshall

Client: Creative Editions

Medium: Colored pencil, watercolor on paper

Size: 10" x 7 1/2"

156

Artist: **ETIENNE DELESSERT**

Art Director: Rita Marshall

Client: Creative Editions

Medium: Colored pencil, watercolor on paper

Size: 10" x 12"

153

154

155

156

157

Artist: **PETER de SÈVE**
Art Director: Ruth Ross
Client: Ballantine Books
Medium: Watercolor, ink on paper
Size: 10" x 8 1/2"

158

Artist: **ANTHONY BROWNE**
Art Director: Lynn Boulton
Client: Turner Publishing, Inc.
Medium: Mixed
Size: 10" x 7"

159

Artist: **MARC BURCKHARDT**
Art Director: Rick Pracher
Client: Grove/Atlantic
Medium: Acrylic on watercolor paper
Size: 12" x 8"

160

Artist: **LOIS EHLERT**
Art Director: Michael Farmer
Client: Harcourt Brace & Co.
Medium: Mixed on paper
Size: 14 1/2" x 23"

157

158

159

160

161
Artist: **DONATO GIANCOLA**
Art Director: Jerry Todd
Client: Penguin USA
Medium: Oil on paper
Size: 32" x 18"

162
Artist: **HENRIK DRESCHER**
Art Director: Ellen Friedman
Client: Hyperion Books for Children
Medium: Watercolor, colored pencil on paper
Size: 10 1/2" x 16 1/2"

163
Artist: **VIVIENNE FLESHER**
Art Director: Lynn Andreozzi
Client: Dell Publishing
Medium: Pastel on paper
Size: 13 1/2" x 10 1/2"

164
Artist: **CHRIS GALL**
Art Director: Nicholas Krenitsky
Client: HarperCollins
Medium: Mixed
Size: 12" x 7"

161

162

163

164

165
Artist: **TRISTAN ELWELL**
Art Director: Tom Egner
Client: Avon Books
Medium: Oil on masonite
Size: 15 1/2" x 9 1/2"

166
Artist: **RAUL COLON**
Art Director: Denise Cronin
Client: Alfred A. Knopf
Medium: Watercolor, colored pencil on paper
Size: 18 1/4" x 15 1/4"

167
Artist: **GARY KELLEY**
Art Director: Gary Kelley
Client: Hearst Center for the Arts
Medium: Pastel on paper
Size: 16" x 12"

168
Artist: **ED LINDLOF**
Art Director: Rich Hendel
Client: University of Hawaii Press
Medium: Rotring colors on Bristol
Size: 15" x 15"

165

166

167

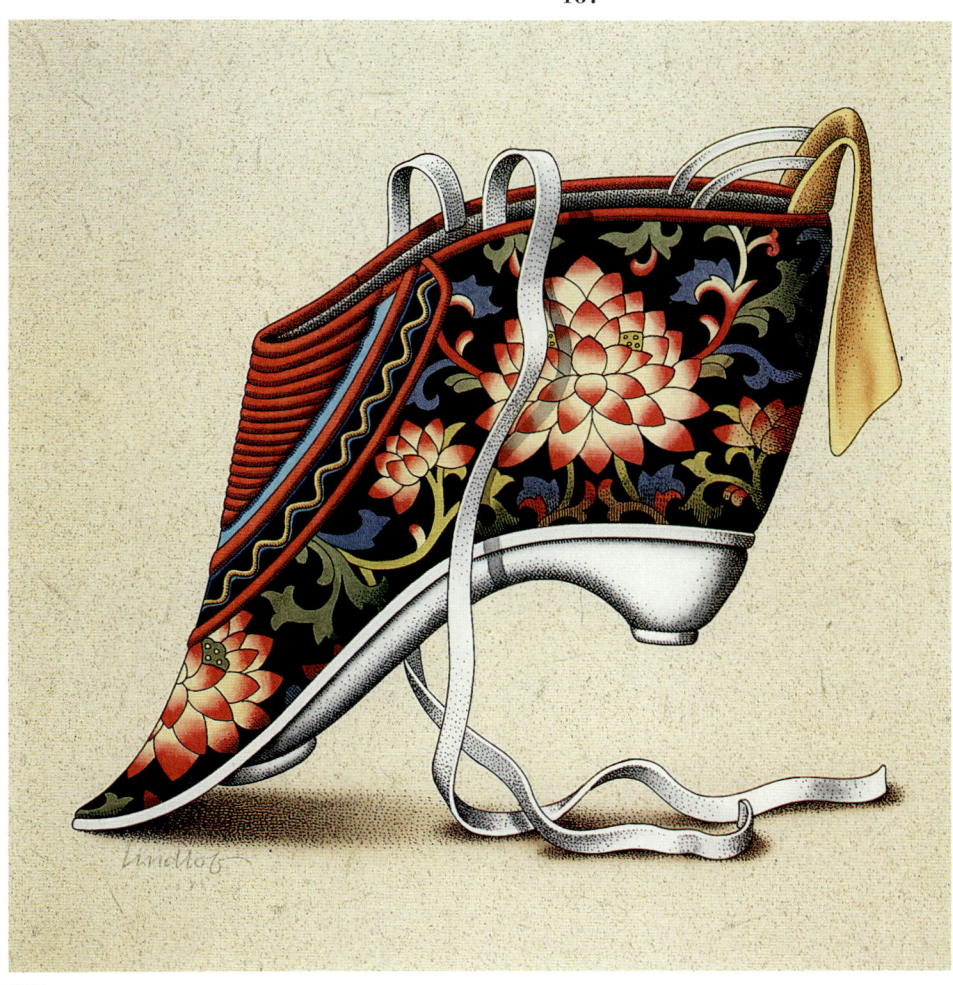

168

169

Artist: **JANET WOOLLEY**

Art Director: Julia Kushnirsky

Client: Warner Books

Medium: Acrylic, photo montage on board

170

Artist: **DAVID SHANNON**

Art Director: Gunta Alexander

Client: Putnam

Medium: Acrylic on board

Size: 13" x 24"

171

Artist: **DANIEL PELAVIN**

Art Director: Nora Wertz

Client: Oxford University Press

Medium: Computer generated

Size: 40" x 30"

172

Artist: **WIKTOR SADOWSKI**

Art Director: Joan Sommers

Client: The University of Chicago Press

Medium: Acrylic on board

169

170

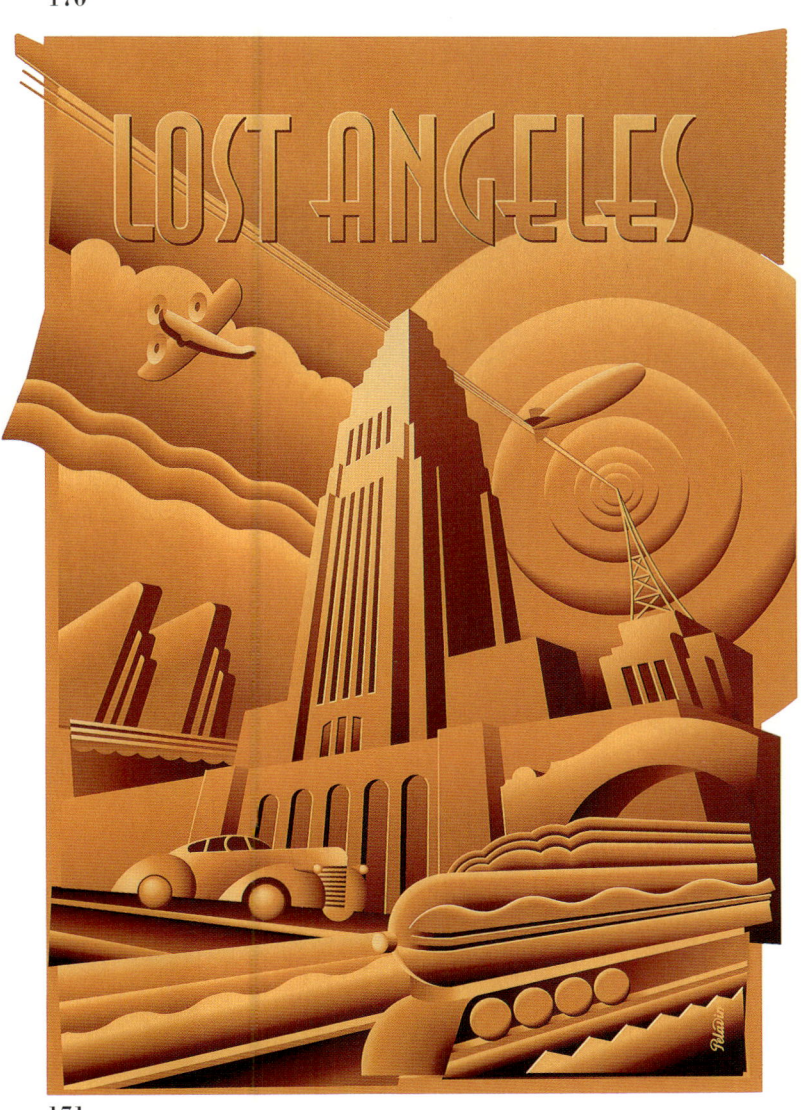

171

172

173

Artist: **SKIP LIEPKE**
Art Director: Skip Liepke
Client: Eleanor Ettinger Gallery
Medium: Watercolor on board
Size: 14" x 20"

174

Artist: **SKIP LIEPKE**
Art Director: Skip Liepke
Client: Eleanor Ettinger Gallery
Medium: Oil on canvas
Size: 26" x 28"

175

Artist: **JOEL PETER JOHNSON**
Art Director: Mark Caleb
Client: Houghton Mifflin
Medium: Oil, acrylic on board
Size: 9" X 8"

176

Artist: **ROBERT CRAWFORD**
Art Director: David Bamford
Client: Berkley Publishing Group
Medium: Acrylic on masonite
Size: 14 1/2" x 11"

173

174

175

176

177

Artist: **MARK ENGLISH**

Art Director: Bruce Hartman

Client: Johnson County Cultural Center

Medium: Oil

Size: 17 1/2" x 23"

178

Artist: **ETIENNE DELESSERT**

Art Director: Rita Marshall

Client: Creative Editions

Medium: Colored pencil, watercolor on paper

Size: 10" x 12"

179

Artist: **JOHN NICKLE**

Art Director: Paolo Pepe

Client: Pocket Books

Medium: Oil, acrylic on board

Size: 18" x 12"

180

Artist: **MICHAEL J. DEAS**

Art Director: George Cornell

Client: Penguin USA

Medium: Oil on panel

Size: 24" x 12 1/2"

177

178

179

180

181
Artist: **MICHAEL KOELSCH**
Art Director: Vaughn Andrews
Client: Harcourt Brace & Co.
Medium: Mixed on board
Size: 17" x 11"

182
Artist: **JERRY PINKNEY**
Art Director: Atha Tehon
Client: Dial Books
Medium: Watercolor, pencil on Arches
Size: 12 3/4" x 17"

183
Artist: **JANET ATKINSON**
Art Director: Henry Sene Yee
Client: St. Martin's Press
Medium: Acrylic on board
Size: 9 1/2" x 7"

184
Artist: **SERGIO MARTINEZ**
Art Directors: Barry Klugerman
              James Warhola
Client: Elfin Light Press
Medium: Colored pencil on paper
Size: 16 3/4" x 12 1/2"

181

182

183

184

185
Artist: **JOYCE PATTI**
Art Director: Mary Bess Engle
Client: Simon & Schuster
Medium: Oil on board
Size: 16" x 10 1/2"

186
Artist: **JERRY PINKNEY**
Art Director: Atha Tehon
Client: Dial Books
Medium: Watercolor, pencil on Arches
Size: 22" x 14 1/2"

187
Artist: **TIM O'BRIEN**
Art Director: Elizabeth B. Parisi
Client: Scholastic Inc.
Medium: Oil on board
Size: 20" x 18"

188
Artist: **MARVIN MATTELSON**
Art Director: George Cornell
Client: New American Library
Medium: Oil on canvas
Size: 13" x 9"

186

187

188

189

Artist: **WILSON McLEAN**
Art Director: Jackie Merri Meyer
Client: Warner Books
Medium: Oil
Size: 26" x 17"

190

Artist: **DAVID SHANNON**
Art Director: Kathy Westray
Client: Scholastic Inc.
Medium: Acrylic on board
Size: 12 1/2" x 23 1/2"

191

Artist: **PHILLIP SINGER**
Art Director: David Tommasino
Client: Scholastic Inc.
Medium: Oil
Size: 16" x 9 1/4"

192

Artist: **DAVID TAMURA**
Art Director: Wendy Bass
Client: Macmillan Inc.
Medium: Oil on masonite
Size: 21" x 18"

190

191

192

193
Artist: **JENNY TYLDEN-WRIGHT**
Art Director: Victor Weaver
Client: Hyperion Books
Medium: Colored pencil on paper
Size: 12" x 8"

194
Artists: **ANDREI DUGIN
OLGA DUGINA**
Art Director: Mathias Berg
Client: Thomasson-Grant
Medium: Watercolor on paper
Size: 13 1/2" x 19"

195
Artist: **YASUTAKA TAGA**
Art Director: Shinichiro Tora
Client: Graphic-Sha, Inc.
Medium: Acrylic on clay sculpture
Size: 18" x 12"

196
Artist: **CATHLEEN TOELKE**
Art Director: Michael Farmer
Client: Harcourt Brace & Co.
Medium: Gouache on board
Size: 9" x 6 1/2"

193

194

195

196

197

Artist: **DANIEL ADEL**

Art Director: Jeri Hansen

Client: Viking Penguin

Medium: Oil on board

Size: 9 ½" X 8"

198

Artist: **CATHLEEN TOELKE**

Art Director: Wendy Bass

Client: Atheneum/Macmillan Publishing Co.

Medium: Gouache on board

Size: 10" x 17"

199

Artist: **ELLEN THOMPSON**

Art Director: Ellen Friedman

Client: Hyperion Books For Children

Medium: Watercolor on Arches

Size: 8" x 5 ½"

200

Artist: **LOIS EHLERT**

Art Director: Tom Starace

Client: HarperCollins

Medium: Watercolor collage on Strathmore

Size: 8" x 22"

197

198

199

200

201

Artist: **JERRY LoFARO**

Art Director: Gail Dubov

Client: Avon Books

Medium: Acrylic on board

Size: 23 ½" x 17 ½"

202

Artist: **BRAD WEINMAN**

Art Director: Vaughn Andrews

Client: Harcourt Brace & Co.

Medium: Oil on paper

203

Artist: **DORIAN VALLEJO**

Art Director: Tom Egner

Client: Avon Books

Medium: Oil

Size: 30" x 20"

204

Artist: **CARLOS ROSADO**

Art Director: Henry Sene Yee

Client: St. Martin's Press

Medium: Oil on masonite

201

202

203

204

205

Artist: **ERIC WHITE**

Art Directors: Rob Weisbach
Eric White

Client: Bantam Books

Medium: Acrylic on Bristol

Size: 6" x 6"

206

Artist: **ERIC WHITE**

Art Directors: Rob Weisbach
Eric White

Client: Bantam Books

Medium: Acrylic on Bristol

Size: 7" x 7"

207

Artist: **CHARLES SANTORE**

Art Directors: Don Bender
Melissa Ring

Client: Random House Value Publishing, Inc.

Medium: Watercolor

208

Artist: **JOHN HERSEY**

Art Director: Simms Taback

Client: Graphic Artists Guild

Medium: Computer generated

205

206

207

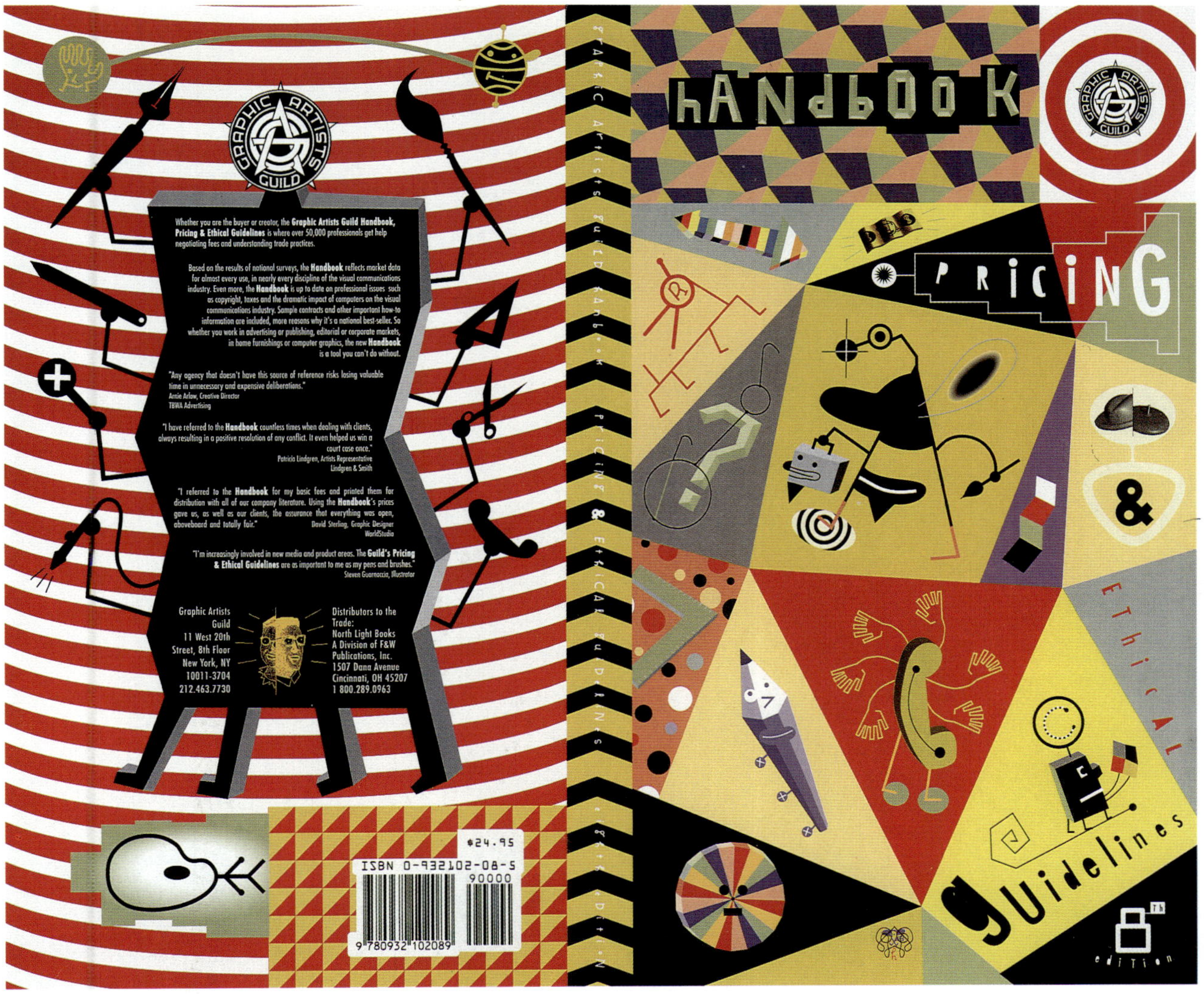

208

209

Artist: **ROBERT CRAWFORD**

Art Director: Joan Sommers

Client: The University of Chicago Press

Medium: Acrylic on masonite

Size: 8" x 8"

210

Artist: **CHRISTINE HERMAN MERRILL**

Art Director: Harriett Barton

Client: HarperCollins

Medium: Oil on canvas

Size: 15 1/2" x 15 1/2"

211

Artist: **MARK SUMMERS**

Art Director: John Kelly

Client: Barnes & Noble

Medium: Scratchboard

Size: 8 1/2" x 11"

212

Artist: **CARTER GOODRICH**

Art Director: Diane Luger

Client: Warner Books

Medium: Colored pencil, watercolor on board

Size: 23" x 16 1/2"

213

Artist: **DUGALD STERMER**

Client: HarperCollins

Medium: Pencil, watercolor on Arches

Size: 14" x 20"

209

210

211

212

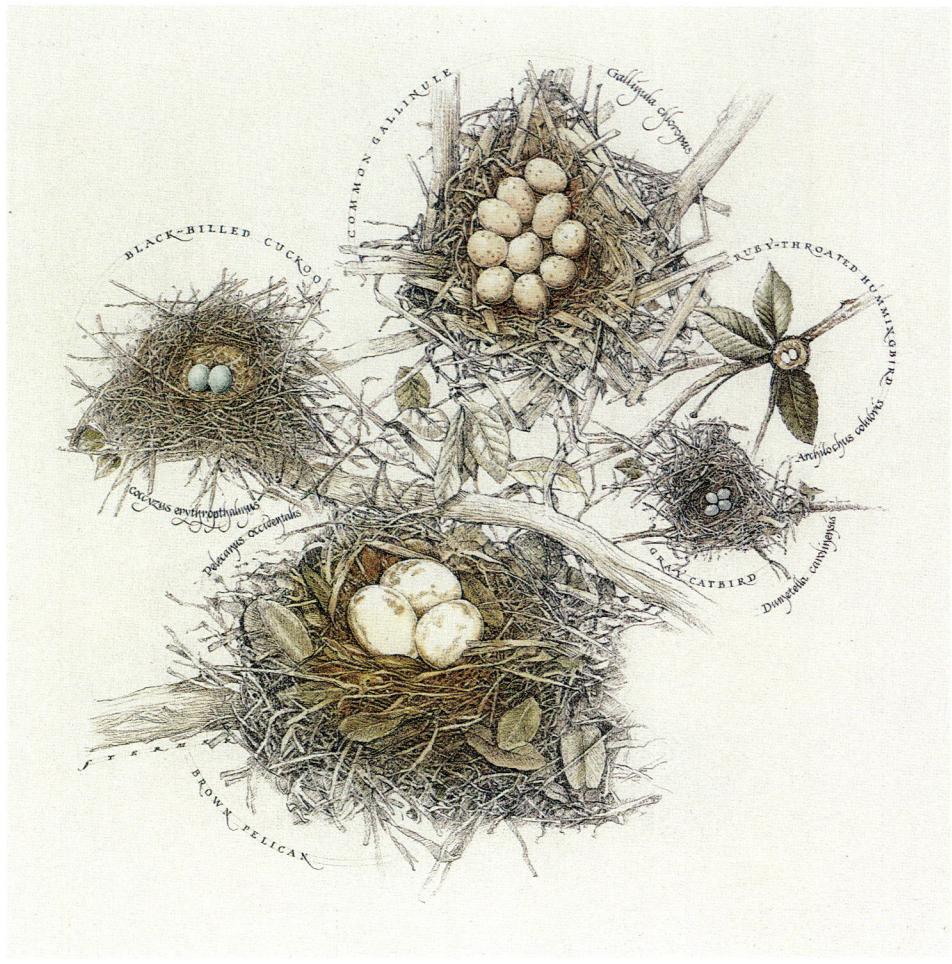
213

214
Artist: **MANUEL P. SANJULIAN**
Art Director: Jerry Counihan
Client: Dell Publishing
Medium: Oil on canvas
Size: 30" x 20"

215
Artist: **JUDY PEDERSEN**
Art Directors: Jean Krules
Jane Byers Bierhorst
Client: Macmillan Inc.
Medium: Mixed
Size: 14 1/4" x 14 1/4"

216
Artist: **ROBERT GIUSTI**
Art Director: Jordi Blassi
Client: Jordi Blassi
Medium: Acrylic on linen
Size: 15 1/2" x 34"

217
Artist: **ROBERT GIUSTI**
Art Director: Jordi Blassi
Client: Jordi Blassi
Medium: Acrylic on canvas
Size: 15 1/2" x 34"

214

215

216

217

218
Artist: **MARK SUMMERS**
Art Director: John Kelly
Client: Barnes & Noble
Medium: Scratchboard
Size: 8 1/2" x 11"

219
Artist: **DAVE McKEAN**
Art Director: Michael Accordino
Client: St. Martin's Press
Medium: Collage

220
Artist: **HENRIK DRESCHER**
Art Director: Ellen Friedman
Client: Hyperion Books for Children
Medium: Watercolor, colored pencil on paper

221
Artist: **MEL ODOM**
Art Director: Steven Brower
Client: Carol Publishing Group
Medium: Pencil, dyes, gouache on board
Size: 10" x 8"

222
Artist: **CHRIS VAN ALLSBURG**
Art Director: Tom Starace
Client: HarperCollins
Medium: Pencil on Croquille board
Size: 18" x 12"

218

219

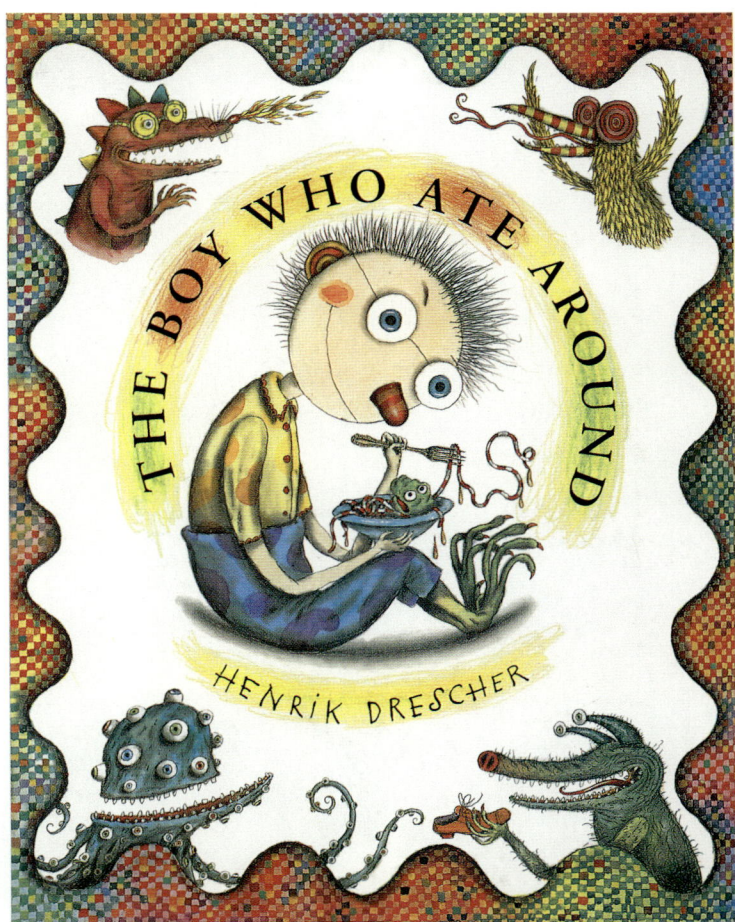

220

221

222

223
Artist: **MARVIN MATTELSON**
Art Director: Richard Lebenson
Client: RSVP
Medium: Oil on ragboard
Size: 10" x 6 1/2"

224
Artist: **ROB WOOD**
Art Director: Neil Stuart
Client: Penguin USA
Medium: Acrylic on board
Size: 17" x 10"

225
Artist: **ROBERT McGINNIS**
Art Director: Joni Friedman
Client: Berkley Publishing Group
Medium: Tempera on masonite
Size: 21 1/2" x 13"

226
Artist: **JILL McELMURRY**
Art Director: Sharon Smith
Client: Mercury House
Medium: Colored pencil on Bristol paper
Size: 7" x 7"

224

225

226

227

Artist: **JOHN JUDE PALENCAR**
Art Director: Judith Murello
Client: Berkley Publishing Group
Medium: Watercolor, acrylic on board
Size: 30" x 20"

228

Artist: **WILLIAM JOYCE**
Art Director: Christine Kettner
Client: HarperCollins
Medium: Oil on Bristol board
Size: 15" x 20"

229

Artist: **YORIKO ITO**
Art Director: Lynn Braswell
Client: Bantam Doubleday Dell
Medium: Mixed
Size: 16 1/2" x 24 1/2"

230

Artist: **H. B. LEWIS**
Art Director: Leslie Bauman
Medium: Mixed
Size: 9 1/2" x 14 1/2"

227

228

231
Artist: **TIM O'BRIEN**
Art Director: Elizabeth B. Parisi
Client: Scholastic Inc.
Medium: Oil on board
Size: 23" x 16"

232
Artist: **DAVID KAHL**
Art Director: Vaughn Andrews
Agency: Clarity Coverdale Fury
Client: Harcourt Brace & Co.
Medium: Digital collage print
Size: 20" x 17"

233
Artist: **DAVID SHANNON**
Art Director: Gunta Alexander
Client: Putnam
Medium: Acrylic on board
Size: 15" x 12"

234
Artist: **DANIEL ADEL**
Art Director: Jeri Hansen
Client: Viking Penguin
Medium: Oil on board
Size: 9" x 9"

BOOK
Illustrators 37

232

233

234

ADVERTISING JURY

RAFAL OLBINSKI
CHAIRMAN
Illustrator

CARY AUSTIN
Illustrator

DWAYNE J. FLINCHUM
Art Director,

ROBERT GOLDSTROM
Illustrator

MARY GRANDPRÉ
Illustrator

MIRKO ILIC
Illustrator

ELIZABETH PARISI
Art Director,
Scholastic Inc.

NEIL STUART
Penguin USA

ADVERTISING

AWARD WINNERS

GREG SPALENKA
Gold Medal

EUGENE HOFFMAN
Silver Medal

SCOTT MCKOWEN
Silver Medal

JACK N. UNRUH
Silver Medal

235

Artist: **GREG SPALENKA**

Art Director: Dee Ann Budney

Agency: Citron Haligman Bedecarré

Client: Open Hand

Medium: Mixed

Size: 28" x 19 ½"

Advertising Gold Medal
GREG SPALENKA

"For the most part, my art concerns itself with social and political themes. I am interested in creating imagery that reflects society and the human condition. I work very hard to touch the spirit of these issues, so that I hope I can produce a piece of art that is not only timely but timeless. I'd like to mention that the organization "Open Hand" provides home-delivered meals to people inflicted with AIDS."

Artist: **EUGENE HOFFMAN**

Art Directors: Bob Coonts
Doug Post

Client: Choice Printing

Medium: Cardboard, 3D

Size: 43 1/2" x 44" x 10"

Advertising Silver Medal
EUGENE HOFFMAN

"These structures have a function and honesty more pure perhaps than any cathedral. They are not a metaphor for wheat...they are wheat itself. The spire, fletch, flying buttresses, saints, choir, vaults, arcade are all present in pure and natural forms. Lacking pretentiousness, the structure is literally a sanctuary for the Eucharist. Elevator (hence to elevate) is indeed an appropriate name and function."

237

Artist: **SCOTT McKOWEN**

Art Director: Scott McKowen

Client: The Acting Company

Medium: Scratchboard

Size. 12" x 7 ½"

Advertising Silver Medal
SCOTT McKOWEN

As a certifiable theatre nut, Scott McKowen was drawn to the theatre-rich area of Stratford, Ontario, where he has lived for the last 14 years following his graduation from Michigan University. He has created several posters for productions by The Acting Company of New York and this medal-winner was for their 30-city tour of *Twelfth Night.* The original drawing was scratchboard and only 12 x 7 inches. Rubyliths were used in overlay to add the color—the resulting offset litho is the final art. Scratchboard is not Scott's sole medium, but it appeals to the American markets. Among his other American theatre clients are the Goodman in Chicago, Arena Stage in Washington, DC, and the Roundabout in New York.

238

Artist: **JACK N. UNRUH**

Art Director: Bob Pullum

Agency: Citron Haligman Bedecarré

Client: AVIA

Medium: Ink, watercolor on Strathmore board

Size: 17 ½" x 13 ½"

Advertising Silver Medal
JACK N. UNRUH

"A foot-in-your-face illustration to match the attitude of the dude wearing it. Too ba[d] this was the last in only a series of three. Thanks Bob, it was great while it lasted."

239
Artist: **BRALDT BRALDS**
Art Director: Arnie Arlow
Agency: TBWA Advertising
Client: Grand Marnier
Medium: Oil on canvas
Size: 20" x 24"

240
Artist: **JOHN DeGRACE**
Medium: Pastel on paper
Size: 25" x 19"

241
Artist: **TOM CURRY**
Art Director: Harold Tackett
Client: Wil Tel
Medium: Acrylic on board
Size: 18" x 12 1/2"

242
Artist: **JOHN CARROLL DOYLE**
Art Director: Norm Kohn
Agency: Norm Kohn Studio
Client: WorldFest
Medium: Oil on canvas
Size: 36" x 5"

239

240

241

242

243

Artist: **GREGORY M. DEARTH**
Art Director: Scott Pettit
Agency: Rhea & Kaiser Advertising, Inc.
Client: Rhone-Poulenc Ag Co.
Medium: Scratchboard, dyes on stat
Size: 11" x 8 1/2"

244

Artist: **ETIENNE DELESSERT**
Art Director: Charlotte Hug
Client: Federation des Cooperatives Migros
Medium: Watercolor, pencil on paper
Size: 7" x 16 1/2"

245

Artist: **GREGORY M. DEARTH**
Art Director: Craig Butler
Client: The Workbook
Medium: Scratchboard, dyes on stat
Size: 9 1/2" x 7"

246

Artist: **JOHN DeGRACE**
Medium: Watercolor on Arches
Size: 24 1/2" x 17 1/2"

243

ADVERTISING
Illustrators 37

244

245

246

247

Artist: **KIM BEHM**
Art Director: Kim Behm
Client: Cedar Falls Chamber of Commerce
Medium: Oil on board, stripped for scanning
Size: 17" x 22"

248

Artist: **ROB DAY**
Art Directors: Bruce Dean
Scott Johnson
Client: Indianapolis Repertory Theatre
Medium: Oil on paper
Size: 20" x 20"

249

Artist: **PAUL COX**
Art Director: Bob Daugherty
Agency: Bader Rutter & Assoc., Inc.
Client: Dow Chemical
Medium: Ink, watercolor on paper
Size: 10" x 18"

250

Artist: **JOHN CARROLL DOYLE**
Client: Erwin Music
Medium: Oil on canvas
Size: 60" x 48"

251

Artist: **DIANA DeSANTIS**
Medium: Pastel on board
Size: 29" x 21"

247

248

249

250

251

252

Artist: **STASYS EIDRIGEVICIUS**

Art Director: James Seacat

Client: Actors Theater of Louisville

Medium: Mixed

Size: 18" x 24"

253

Artist: **JOSEPH DANIEL FIEDLER**

Art Director: Corey Glickman

Client: WQED 13

Medium: Alkyd on paper

Size: 15" x 15"

254

Artist: **DAVID LANCE GOINES**

Art Director: David Lance Goines

Client: Iowa Alliance For Arts Education

Medium: Mixed

Size: 22" x 16"

255

Artist: **BASCOVE**

Art Director: Jim Plumeri

Client: Bantam Books

Medium: Oil on canvas

Size: 11 1/2" x 7 1/2"

256

Artist: **JOSEPH DANIEL FIEDLER**

Art Director: Corey Glickman

Client: WQED FM

Medium: Alkyd on paper

Size: 5" x 16"

252

253

254

255

256

257

Artist: **DANIEL CRAIG**
Art Director: Sam Macuga
Client: American Cyanamid
Medium: Oil
Size: 21" x 15"

258

Artist: **MILTON GLASER**
Client: Tomato
Medium: Ink, watercolor on paper
Size: 16 1/2" x 22"

259

Artist: **LISA FRENCH**
Art Director: Mick Kuisel
Client: Outrigger Hotels Hawaii
Medium: Pencil on board
Size: 14" x 10"

260

Artist: **STEVE ELLIS**
Art Director: Marvin Mattelson
Medium: Oil on board
Size: 12 1/2" x 9 1/2"

257

ADVERTISING
Illustrators 37

258

259

260

261

Artist: **KEITH GRAVES**

Art Director: Neal Zimmerman

Agency: Zimmerman Crowe Design

Client: Nature Co.

Medium: Prismacolor, ink on board

Size: 23" x 16 1/2"

262

Artist: **BRAD GOODELL**

Art Directors: Linda Von Boetticher
Leigh Von Boetticher

Client: 20/30 Club Equestrian Fundraiser

Medium: Acrylic, airbrush on board

Size: 11" x 25"

263

Artist: **VIVIENNE FLESHER**

Art Director: Shin Matsunaga

Client: Shiseido

Medium: Pastel on paper

Size: 12" x 12"

264

Artist: **MELINDA BECK**

Medium: Mixed

Size: 13 1/2" x 13 1/2"

261

ADVERTISING
Illustrators 37

262

263

264

265

Artist: **MARK ENGLISH**

Art Director: Jim Plumeri

Client: Bantam Books

Medium: Oil

Size: 9" x 13 1/2"

266

Artist: **CORBERT GAUTHIER**

Art Director: Becky Bjornson

Client: Lifetouch Publishing

Medium: Oil on gessoed board

Size: 17 1/2" x 27"

267

Artist: **ALAN WITSCHONKE**

Art Director: Lilla Rogers

Medium: Oil on board

Size: 7 1/2" x 7 1/2"

268

Artist: **ERIC WHITE**

Art Directors: Eric White
Neil Harris

Client: London/Polygram

Medium: Acrylic on Bristol

Size: 9" x 9"

265

ADVERTISING
Illustrators 37

266

267

268

269

Artist: **GARY KELLEY**

Art Director: Lori McFadden

Client: Eddie Bauer

Medium: Pastel on paper

Size: 19 1/2" x 15 1/2"

270

Artist: **JERRY LoFARO**

Art Director: Scott Brooks

Agency: Q1 Communicators

Client: Ariel Inc.

Medium: Acrylic on board

Size: 10 1/2" x 12 1/2"

271

Artist: **JASON HOLLY**

Art Director: Mary Maurer

Client: Sony Music

Medium: Acrylic on canvas board

Size: 14" x 14"

272

Artist: **JAMES McMULLAN**

Art Director: Belle How

Client: Simpson Paper

Medium: Watercolor on paper

Size: 8 1/2" x 6 1/2"

270

271

272

273
Artist: **JOHN H. HOWARD**
Art Director: Tom Grosspietsch
Client: Cellular One
Medium: Acrylic on canvas
Size: 40" x 30"

274
Artist: **JOHN JINKS**
Art Director: Tracy Bacilek
Client: Perrier
Medium: Acrylic on board
Size: 25" x 36"

275
Artist: **JOHN H. HOWARD**
Art Directors: Mark Burdett
　　　　　　　Stacy Drummond
Client: Sony Music
Medium: Acrylic on canvas
Size: 40" x 30"

276
Artist: **LOIS HATCHER**
Art Director: Bill Ost
Agency: Valentine Radford, Inc.
Client: Ambassador Cards
Medium: Collage of greeting cards on studio floor
Size: 12' x 9'

273

274

275

276

277

Artist: **GREGORY MANCHESS**
Art Director: Matt Reinhard
Agency: Foote Cone & Belding
Client: Killian's Red Beer
Medium: Oil on gesso
Size: 24" x 32 1/2"

278

Artist: **MELISSA GRIMES**
Art Director: M. P. Nourzad
Agency: Franklin & Nourzad
Client: Live Oak Theater
Medium: Color copies, collage and leaves
Size: 22" x 22"

279

Artist: **JOHN RUSH**
Client: The Eleanor Ettinger Gallery
Medium: Oil on canvas
Size: 22" x 32"

280

Artist: **JAMES McMULLAN**
Art Director: Janice Brunell
Agency: Russek Advertising Inc.
Client: Lincoln Center Theater
Medium: Watercolor on paper
Size: 18 1/2" x 11"

281

Artist: **KEITH GRAVES**
Art Director: Neal Zimmerman
Agency: Zimmerman Crowe Design
Client: Nature Co.
Medium: Prismacolor, ink on board
Size: 20" x 12"

277

278

279

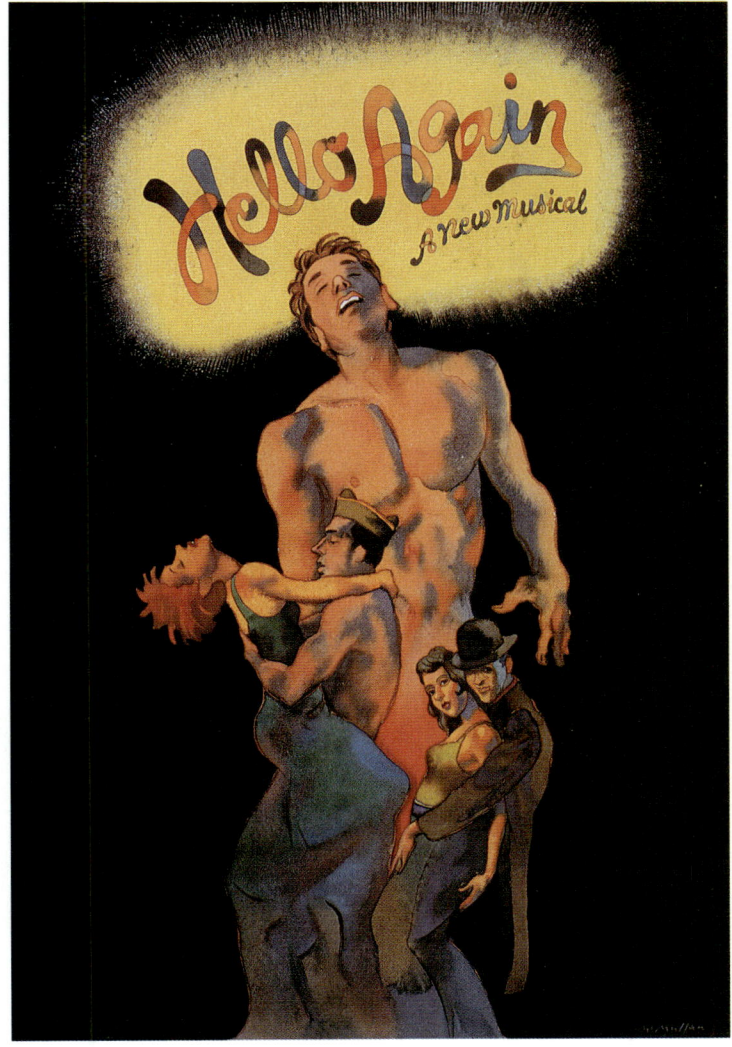

280

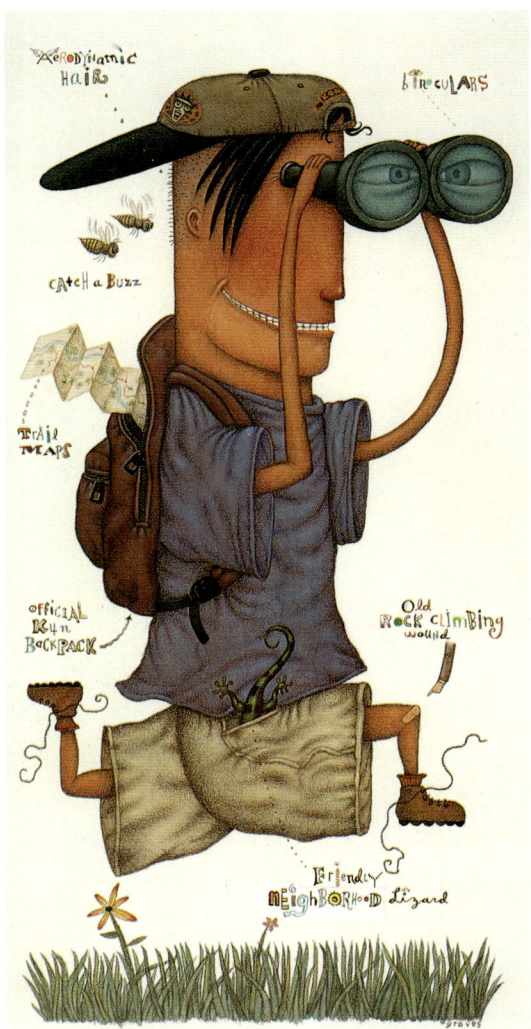

281

282
Artist: **DANIEL CRAIG**
Art Director: Jac Coverdale
Client: Northwestern National Life
Medium: Oil on ragboard
Size: 24" x 16"

283
Artist: **GREGORY M. DEARTH**
Art Director: Kevin Kehoe
Agency: Williams & Rockwood
Client: Zions Bank
Medium: Scratchboard, India ink
Size: 15 1/2" x 10 1/2"

284
Artist: **HAYES HENDERSON**
Art Director: David Ekizian
Agency: Ekizian Design
Client: The Bon Marché
Medium: Oil on paper
Size: 16" x 7 1/2"

285
Artist: **MARK GARRO**
Art Directors: Joe Volpicelli
Jonathan Shlafer
Mike Comisky
Agency: Earthquake NYC
Client: Warner Brothers
Medium: Acrylic on board
Size: 19" x 19 1/2"

282

283

284

285

286
Artist: **BRAD HOLLAND**
Art Director: Guy Marino
Agency: Merkley, Newman & Harty
Client: Bankers Trust
Medium: Acrylic on masonite
Size: 15" x 15"

287
Artist: **BRAD HOLLAND**
Art Director: Erwin Piplits
Client: Serapions Theatre
Medium: Acrylic on board
Size: 19 1/2" x 15 1/2"

288
Artist: **WIKTOR SADOWSKI**
Art Director: Pam Racs
Client: Mark Taper Forum
Medium: Acrylic on cardboard
Size: 18" x 13"

289
Artist: **RANDALL ROYTER**
Art Directors: Eric Bute
Andrew Wallace
Client: F.J.C. and N.
Medium: Acrylic on board
Size: 17" x 21"

286

287

288

289

290
Artist: **BILL NELSON**
Art Director: Greg Crossley
Agency: Farago Advertising Inc.
Client: Image Bank/Film
Medium: Colored pencil on matt board
Size: 19" x 13"

291
Artist: **TONY NOVAK**
Art Director: Richard Nead
Client: Robins, Kaplan, Miller & Ciresi
Medium: Acrylic on board
Size: 20 1/2" x 14"

292
Artist: **C. F. PAYNE**
Art Director: Gary Greenberg
Agency: Rossin, Greenberg, Seronick
Client: Stratus
Medium: Mixed
Size: 16" x 12"

293
Artist: **GENE SPARKMAN**
Client: Art Students League of New York
Medium: Pastel on paper
Size: 19" x 29 1/2"

290

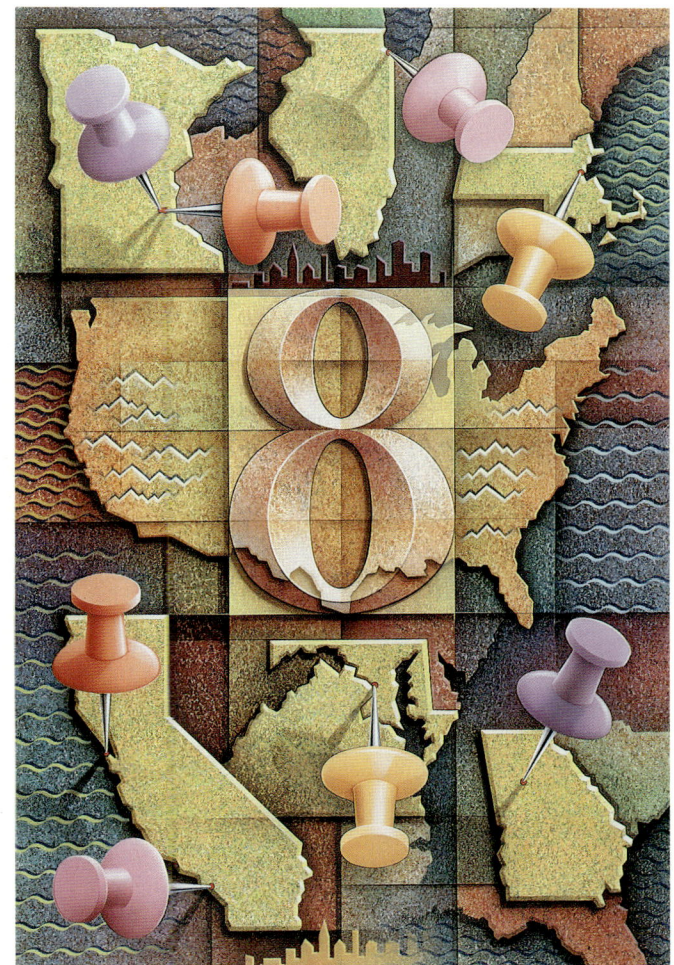

291

292

293

294

Artist: **TIM O'BRIEN**
Art Director: Clifton Lin
Agency: Sive Young & Rubicam
Client: Rainforest Alliance
Medium: Oil on board
Size: 19 1/2" x 12 1/2"

295

Artist: **JOHN RUSH**
Art Director: John Rush
Client: Branson Theater L.P.
Medium: Oil on canvas
Size: 21 1/2" x 31 1/2"

296

Artist: **RAFAL OLBINSKI**
Art Director: Salvatore Garguilo
Client: New York City Opera
Medium: Acrylic on canvas
Size: 20" x 14"

297

Artist: **ADAM MATHEWS**
Medium: Acrylic
Size: 22" x 16"

295

296

297

298
Artist: **GEORGE PRATT**
Art Director: John Rafferty
Client: K. D'Addario
Medium: Oil on linen
Size: 22" x 24"

299
Artist: **BILL MAYER**
Art Director: Mick Kesel
Agency: Lintas Campbell Ewald
Client: Outrigger Hotels Hawaii
Medium: Airbrush on board
Size: 10" x 11"

300
Artist: **MARK RYDEN**
Art Director: David Bartels
Agency: Bartels, Inc.
Client: GDS
Medium: Oil on board
Size: 15" x 30"

301
Artist: **WIKTOR SADOWSKI**
Art Directors: Irene Lewis
Nina Stack
Client: Center Stage
Medium: Acrylic on board

302
Artist: **WIKTOR SADOWSKI**
Art Directors: Irene Lewis
Nina Stack
Client: Center Stage
Medium: Acrylic on board
Size: 18" x 12"

298

299

300

301

302

303
Artist: **RUSS WILSON**
Art Director: Russ Wilson
Client: Jacksonville Convention and Visitors Bureau
Medium: Pastel on paper
Size: 28" x 19"

304
Artist: **MARK SUMMERS**
Art Director: John Parkinson
Client: Ford Motor Co.
Medium: Scratchboard
Size: 6 1/2" x 14 1/2"

305
Artist: **CHRISTOPHER BALDWIN**
Art Director: John Zimmerman
Agency: The Z Group
Client: Beacon Magazine
Medium: Cut Amberlith-mechanical for screen printing
Size: 18" x 23"

306
Artist: **ERIC T. YANG**
Art Director: Andrew Lopez
Client: Bugle Boy Industries
Medium: Screen printing on cotton
Size: 9" x 8"

303

304

305

306

307
Artist: **WILL WILSON**
Art Director: John Lyle Sanford
Client: Discovery Communications Inc.
Medium: Oil on wood panel
Size: 16 1/2" x 11 1/2"

308
Artist: **VICTOR STABIN**
Art Director: Victor Stabin
Client: 29th St. Theater Co.
Medium: Photo Xerox, acrylic, blowtorch on paper
Size: 20" x 14"

309
Artist: **DAVID SLONIM**
Art Directors: Steve Mitchell
Tim Jones
Client: Focus on the Family
Medium: Acrylic on paper
Size: 14" x 10"

310
Artist: **MARCO J. VENTURA**
Art Director: Angelo Sganzerla
Client: Flou
Medium: Oil on paper
Size: 13 1/2" x 20"

307

308

309

310

311

Artist: **BILL MAYER**

Art Director: Mick Kesel

Agency: Lintas Campbell Ewald

Client: Outrigger Hotels Hawaii

Medium: Airbrush on board

Size: 16" x 12"

312

Artist: **RANDALL ROYTER**

Art Director: Randy Stroman

Client: F.J.C. and N.

Medium: Acrylic on board

Size: 12 1/2" x 17"

313

Artists: **STEVE JOHNSON
LOU FANCHER**

Art Director: Jill Savini

Agency: CKS Partners

Client: Norwegian Cruise Line

Medium: Acrylic on paper

Size: 19 1/2" x 13 1/2"

314

Artist: **JAMES McMULLAN**

Art Director: Jim Russek

Agency: Russek Advertising, Inc.

Client: Lincoln Center Theater

Medium: Watercolor, gouache on paper

Size: 10 1/2" x 5 1/2"

315

Artist: **BRALDT BRALDS**

Art Directors: Sue Wierdon
Arnie Arlow

Client: Carillon Importers

Medium: Oil on masonite

Size: 20" x 24"

311

312

313

314

315

316

Artist: **JOHN RUSH**
Art Director: Steve Thompson
Agency: Traverrohback Inc.
Client: Johnson Controls, Inc.
Medium: Gouache on gessoed linen board
Size: 18" x 18"

317

Artist: **MARY GRANDPRÉ**
Art Director: Craig Butler
Client: The Workbook
Medium: Pastel on paper
Size: 19 1/2" x 15"

318

Artist: **KAZUHIKO SANO**
Art Directors: David Golden
Laurie Carver
Agency: Hamilton, Carver & Lee
Client: Du Pont Pharmaceuticals
Medium: Acrylic
Size: 17" x 14"

319

Artist: **MICHAEL PARASKEVAS**
Art Director: Michael Paraskevas
Client: Lindgren & Smith
Medium: Acrylic on canvas
Size: 28" x 43"

316

317

318

319

320

Artist: **DAN MARSHALL**
Art Director: Dan Marshall
Agency: Marshall Jaccoma Mitchell
Client: A&E Networks,
    The History Channel
Medium: Computer generated
Size: 10 1/2" x 16 1/2"

321

Artist: **DALE CRAWFORD**
Art Director: Angie Hurlbut
Client: The Business Information Group
Medium: Acrylic on Bristol
Size: 12" x 8 1/2"

322

Artist: **MARVIN MATTELSON**
Art Director: Jay Barbieri
Client: Angel Records/EMI Classics
Medium: Oil
Size: 8" x 8"

323

Artist: **LESLIE ROBERTS**
Medium: Colored pencil on Bristol board
Size: 11 1/2" x 15"

320

321

322

323

INSTITUTIONAL JURY

**C.F. PAYNE
CHAIRMAN**
Illustrator

PAMELA EITZEN
Associate, The Creative Department, Inc.

COLIN FORBES
Consulting Partner, Pentagram Design

AL LORENZ
Illustrator

RICHARD MERKIN
*Painter/Illustrator/
Teacher/Archivist*

JOHN JUDE PALENCAR
Illustrator

JOHN RUSH
Illustrator

CATHLEEN TOELKE
Illustrator

JESSICA WEBER
*President,
Jessica Weber Design, Inc.*

INSTITUTIONAL

AWARD WINNERS

MIKE BENNY
Gold Medal

JOHN COLLIER
Gold Medal

ETIENNE DELESSERT
Gold Medal

VIVIENNE FLESHER
Silver Medal

GARY KELLEY
Silver Medal

INSTITUTIONAL
Illustrators 37

324

Artist: **MIKE BENNY**
Art Director: Bob Beyn
Agency: Seraphein Beyn
Medium: Acrylic on board
Size: 17" x 27 1/2"

Institutional Gold Medal
MIKE BENNY

"A graduate of Chico State, California, in graphic design, I have worked as an illustrator full time for six years. This illustration was used for an annual poster project I've done for Seraphein Beyn Advertising for the last five years. They specialize in car dealership ads, thus their slogan: "Hard Hitting Advertising." With 365 days to work on this project, I faithfully allot the final four days to begin."

324

325

Artist: **JOHN COLLIER**

Art Directors: Wendy Batteau, Louise Fili

Client: Macmillan Inc.

Medium: Pastel on paper

Size: 23" x 21"

Institutional Gold Medal
JOHN COLLIER

John Collier was chosen by Macmillan to do this 1995 Edith Wharton calendar. The images are Collier's interpretations of notable Wharton quotes. One of the difficulties, he says, was to bring fresh ideas to each and to see each through 20th century eyes. A stroke of serendipity did occur in his research for period costumes. He came across the drama department of Southern Methodist University in his hometown of Dallas. And, with student actresses as models, he was set.

Artist: **ETIENNE DELESSERT**
Art Director: Etienne Delessert
Client: Galerie Vallotton
Medium: Acrylic on tin
Size: 20" x 18"

Institutional Gold Medal
ETIENNE DELESSERT

This image was one of 30 which Etienne Delessert created for the catalogue and poster for his gallery in Lausanne, Switzerland. The theme, in translation, is "Little Bits of Paradise." The artist explains that we are all in the dark and only illuminated by a touch of light…just as paradise is only those wonderful precious moments that occur during a long, arduous day. He used acrylics on flat sheets of tin which he had come across at Seymour Chwast's studio.

327

Artist: **VIVIENNE FLESHER**

Art Directors: **Patrick Coyne, Paul Elliot**

Client: **Communication Arts/ Rabbit Ears**

Medium: **Pastel on paper**

Size: **15" x 22 ½"**

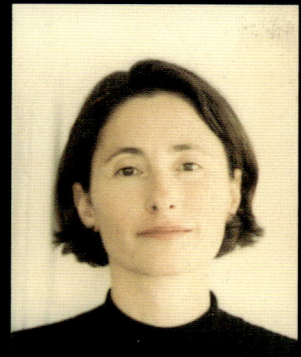

Institutional Silver Medal
VIVIENNE FLESHER

"I enjoyed drawing the girl wrapped in the gold wing. I think the judges saw that. Paul Elliott and Craig Rodgers at Rabbit Ears know how to work with illustrators, therefore, they get the very best from the artists they work with."

INSTITUTIONAL
Illustrators 37

Institutional Silver Medal
GARY KELLEY

"Fortunately, at this point in my life as an illustrator, many more assignment Beauties than are Beasts. This was one of those assignments. The art direct me to do the poster, trusted me to do it right, and got out of the way. That's the work. Thanks."

329

Artist: **ALAN E. COBER**

Art Director: Alisann Marshall

Client: American Way

Medium: Etching, hand colored on Arches cover

Size: 11 1/2" x 8 1/2"

330

Artist: **ALAN E. COBER**

Art Directors: Sheri Squires
Denise Olding

Client: The Louisville Graphic Design Assoc.

Medium: Etching, aquatint on German etching paper

Size: 16" x 19 1/2"

331
Artist: **LONNIE BUSCH**
Art Director: Dorothy Krygier
Client: MBI
Medium: Airbrush
Size: 11" x 15"

332
Artist: **BRYN BARNARD**
Art Director: Bryn Barnard
Client: New Jersey State Council on the Arts
Medium: Oil on linen
Size: 18" x 15"

333
Artist: **DON ARDAY**
Art Director: Mark Greer
Client: Memorial Healthcare System
Medium: Computer generated
Size: 8" x 6 1/2"

334
Artist: **DON ASMUSSEN**
Medium: Pen & ink, watercolor collage
Size: 22" x 16"

331

INSTITUTIONAL
Illustrators 37

332

333

334

335
Artist: **JAMES BENNETT**
Medium: Oil on board
Size: 13" x 12"

336
Artist: **JAMES BENNETT**
Medium: Oil on board
Size: 8" x 15"

337
Artist: **THOM ANG**
Art Director: Gary Gerani
Client: The Topps Co., Inc.
Medium: Mixed on paper
Size: 11" x 8 1/2"

338
Artist: **THOMAS BLACKSHEAR**
Art Director: David Usher
Client: The Greenwich Workshop
Medium: Oil on canvas
Size: 33" x 26"

335

336

337

338

339

Artist: **JAMES GURNEY**

Art Director: David Usher

Client: The Greenwich Workshop

Medium: Oil on canvas

Size: 14 1/2" x 15"

340

Artist: **JAMES GURNEY**

Art Director: David Usher

Client: The Greenwich Workshop

Medium: Oil on canvas

Size: 14" x 15"

341

Artist: **MIKE BENNY**

Art Directors: Tony Lentini
John Weaver
Gluth Weaver

Agency: Gluth Weaver

Client: Mitchell Energy Development Corp.

Medium: Acrylic on board

Size: 16" x 20"

342

Artist: **MIKE BENNY**

Art Directors: Tony Lentini
John Weaver
Gluth Weaver

Agency: Gluth Weaver

Client: Mitchell Energy Development Corp.

Medium: Acrylic on board

Size: 16" x 20"

339

340

341

342

343

Artist: **MALCOLM FARLEY**

Art Director: Malcolm Farley

Client: Tumbleweed Press

Medium: Mixed on board

Size: 16" x 16"

344

Artist: **JOHN FERRY**

Medium: Oil on masonite

Size: 7" x 7"

345

Artist: **MICHAEL J. DEAS**

Art Director: Carl Herrman

Client: Carl Herrman

Medium: Oil on paper

Size: 4" x 8"

346

Artist: **VIVIENNE FLESHER**

Art Directors: Partick Coyne
Paul Elliot

Client: Communication Arts/
Rabbit Ears

Medium: Pastel on paper

Size: 30" x 34"

347

Artist: **BART FORBES**

Art Director: Murray Tinkelman

Medium: Oil on canvas

Size: 20" x 14"

343

344

345

346

347

348
Artist: **SUZANNE DURANCEAU**
Art Director: Suzanne Duranceau
Client: Sunrise Publications Inc.
Medium: Acrylic on board
Size: 14" x 10"

349
Artist: **VIVIENNE FLESHER**
Art Director: Debra Flynn-Hanrahan
Client: The Atlantic Monthly
Medium: Pastel on paper
Size: 10" x 8 1/2"

350
Artist: **BART FORBES**
Client: Bruce McGaw Graphics
Medium: Oil on canvas
Size: 38" x 15 1/2"

351
Artist: **JOHN ENGLISH**
Art Director: Sharyn O'Mara
Agency: Studio'Mara
Client: The Raphael Hotel Group
Medium: Oil on canvas
Size: 19" x 15 1/2"

349

351

350

352
Artist: **JAMES GURNEY**
Art Director: David Usher
Client: The Greenwich Workshop
Medium: Oil on canvas
Size: 35 1/2" x 23 1/2"

353
Artist: **WILL HILLENBRAND**
Art Director: Will Hillenbrand
Client: Champion International Corp.
Medium: Oil on linen
Size: 23" x 30"

354
Artist: **ROBERT M. CUNNINGHAM**
Art Director: Jennifer Lawson
Client: L.L. Bean
Medium: Acrylic on paper
Size: 20 1/2" x 18 1/2"

355
Artist: **MARY GRANDPRÉ**
Art Director: Mary GrandPré
Client: Scott Hull Assoc.
Medium: Pastel on paper
Size: 19" x 14 1/2"

INSTITUTIONAL
Illustrators 37

353

354

355

356
Artist: **DAVID BOWERS**
Medium: Oil on masonite
Size: 14" x 11"

357
Artist: **ROBERT GIUSTI**
Art Director: Mark Hess
Client: The Newborn Group
Medium: Acrylic on canvas
Size: 24 1/2" x 16 1/2"

358
Artist: **JOHN H. HOWARD**
Art Director: Franka Melis
Agency: BUH Communicatie Adviesbureau
Client: GTI
Medium: Acrylic on canvas
Size: 22" x 30"

359
Artist: **ANN GLOVER**
Medium: Oil on panel
Size: 6" x 9"

356

INSTITUTIONAL
Illustrators 37

357

358

359

360
Artist: **GARY KELLEY**
Art Director: S. Stagmeister
Client: Four Seasons Hotel
Medium: Pastel on paper
Size: 30" x 36"

361
Artist: **WILSON McLEAN**
Art Director: Shoji Matsuzaki
Client: Shoji Matsuzaki
Medium: Oil on canvas
Size: 27 1/2" x 28"

362
Artist: **PAUL LEE**
Client: Sarah Bain Gallery
Medium: Acrylic on board
Size: 16 1/2" x 11 1/2"

363
Artist: **THEO RUDNAK**
Art Director: Lynn Phelps
Client: AIGA/Minnesota
Medium: Gouache on watercolor rag
Size: 58" x 13 1/2"

364
Artist: **ANITA KUNZ**
Art Director: Sunil Bhandari
Agency: Harris & Bhandari
Medium: Watercolor, gouache on board
Size: 13" x 10"

360

361

INSTITUTIONAL
Illustrators 37

362

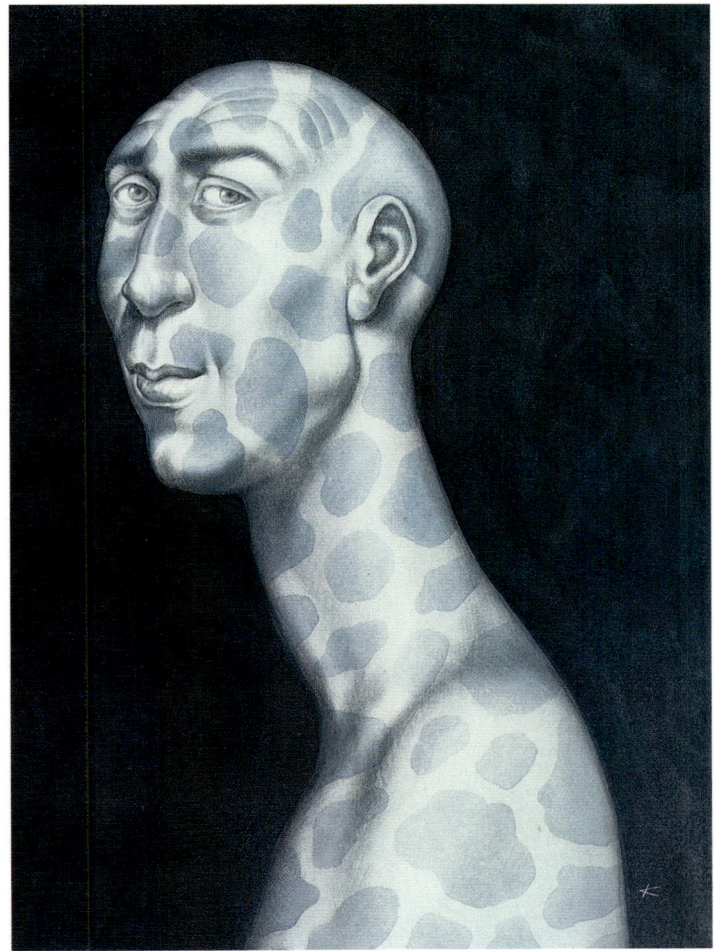

364

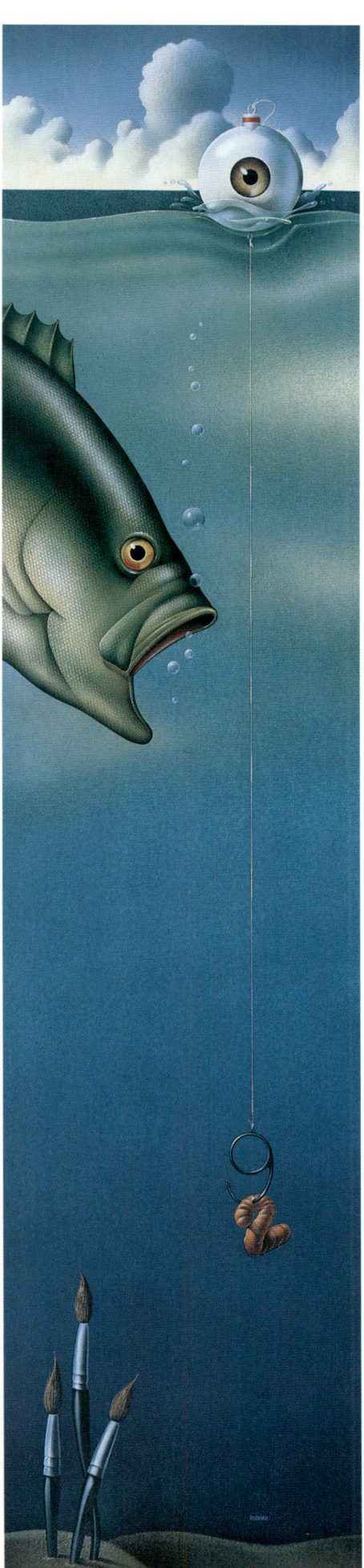

363

365

Artist: **GARY LOCKE**
Art Director: Clay Turner
Agency: Ackerman McQueen
Client: NRA
Medium: Watercolor, colored pencil, pastel
Size: 14" x 10 1/2"

366

Artist: **JOHN CLAPP**
Medium: Watercolor on paper
Size: 8" x 12"

367

Artist: **DAVE LA FLEUR**
Medium: Oil on canvas
Size: 8" x 22 1/2"

368

Artist: **JIM PAUL**
Art Director: Jim Paul
Client: Hallmark Cards
Medium: Mixed on paper
Size: 9" x 5 1/2"

369

Artist: **STEVEN POLSON**
Art Director: Bill Borman
Agency: Borman Communications
Client: Grand Lodge of New York
Medium: Oil on canvas
Size: 16" x 13 1/2"

365

366

367

368

369

370

Artist: **GREGORY MANCHESS**
Art Director: Richard Solomon
Client: Richard Solomon Artists Representative
Medium: Oil on gesso
Size: 25" x 33 1/2"

371

Artist: **DAVID JOHNSON**
Art Director: Paul Elliot
Client: Rabbit Ears Productions
Medium: Pen & ink, watercolor on paper
Size: 15" x 22"

372

Artist: **JOHN P. MAGGARD III**
Art Directors: Cliff Schwandner
Kris Schwandner
Client: Cincinnati Heart Assoc.
Medium: Acrylic, ink on Strathmore
Size: 24 1/2" x 11"

373

Artist: **ALAN E. COBER**
Art Director: Alisann Marshall
Client: American Way
Medium: Etching, hand colored on Arches cover
Size: 10" x 7"

374

Artist: **GREGORY M. DEARTH**
Art Director: Laura Jones
Agency: Littleton 2
Client: Scott Hull Assoc.
Medium: Scratchboard, ink
Size: 11 1/2" x 9"

370

371

372

373

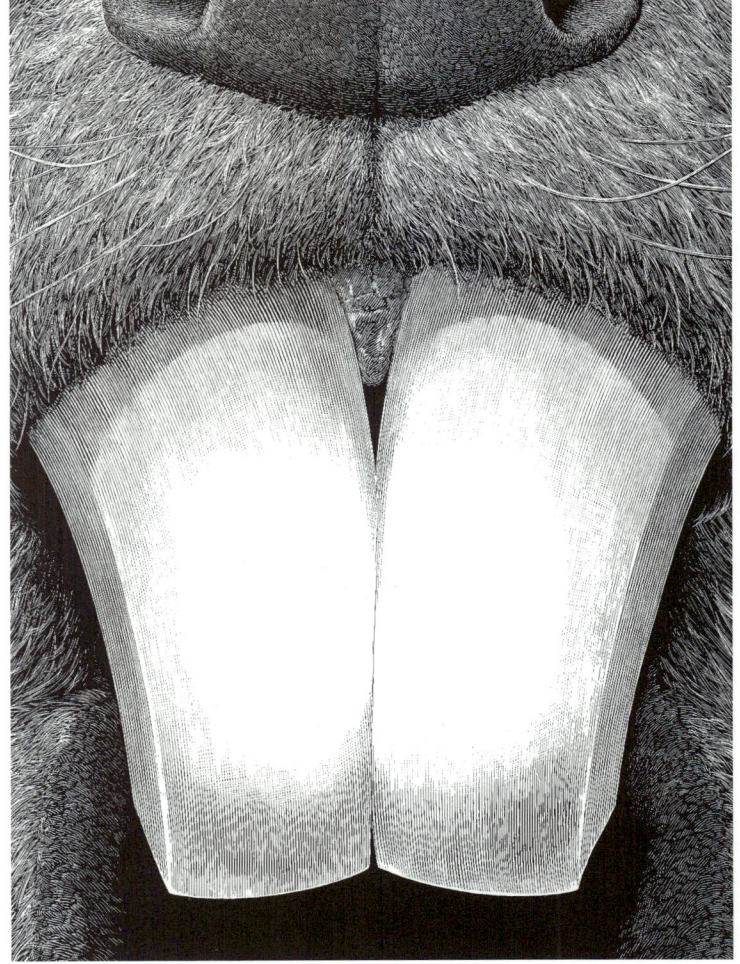

374

375
Artist: **RAFAL OLBINSKI**
Art Director: Cathryn Mezzo
Client: P.S.J. Warsaw
Medium: Acrylic on canvas
Size: 30" x 22"

376
Artist: **GREGORY MANCHESS**
Art Director: Sherri Witham
Client: Witham Fine Art
Medium: Oil on linen
Size: 32" x 24 1/2"

377
Artist: **GREGORY MANCHESS**
Art Director: Richard Solomon
Client: Richard Solomon Artists Representative
Medium: Oil on gesso
Size: 18" x 14"

378
Artist: **SERGIO MARTINEZ**
Art Directors: Barry Klugerman
James Warhola
Client: Elfin Light Press
Medium: Mixed
Size: 13 1/2" x 20"

375

376

377

378

379
Artist: **DAVID W. MEIKLE**
Art Director: Scott Greer
Client: Continuing Education/ University of Utah
Medium: Acrylic, etching on paper
Size: 9" x 9"

380
Artist: **DAVID W. MEIKLE**
Art Director: Scott Greer
Agency: DCE Design
Client: Continuing Education/ University of Utah
Medium: Acrylic, etching on paper
Size: 9 1/2" x 9 1/2"

381
Artist: **JOHN THOMPSON**
Art Director: Darwin Bahm
Client: Darwin Bahm
Medium: Acrylic on wood
Size: 11 1/2" x 17 1/2"

382
Artist: **ROBERT NEUBECKER**
Art Director: Ron Stucky
Client: WordPerfect
Medium: Watercolor, ink on paper
Size: 12 1/2" x 9 1/2"

383
Artist: **RAFAL OLBINSKI**
Art Director: Jan Ohye
Client: New York City Opera
Medium: Acrylic on canvas
Size: 20" x 14"

379

380

381

382

383

384

Artist: **JACK N. UNRUH**

Art Director: Jerry McPhail

Client: Women's Guild of United Cerebral Palsy

Medium: Ink, watercolor on Strathmore

Size: 20" x 15"

385

Artist: **JACK N. UNRUH**

Art Director: Michael Bierut

Client: Mohawk Paper

Medium: Ink, watercolor on Strathmore board

Size: 11" x 14"

386

Artist: **JACK N. UNRUH**

Art Director: Ken Koester

Client: Dallas Society of Visual Communications

Medium: Ink, watercolor on Strathmore board

Size: 21 1/2" x 15 1/2"

387

Artist: **JOSÉ ORTEGA**

Medium: Mixed

Size: 9 1/2" x 7"

385

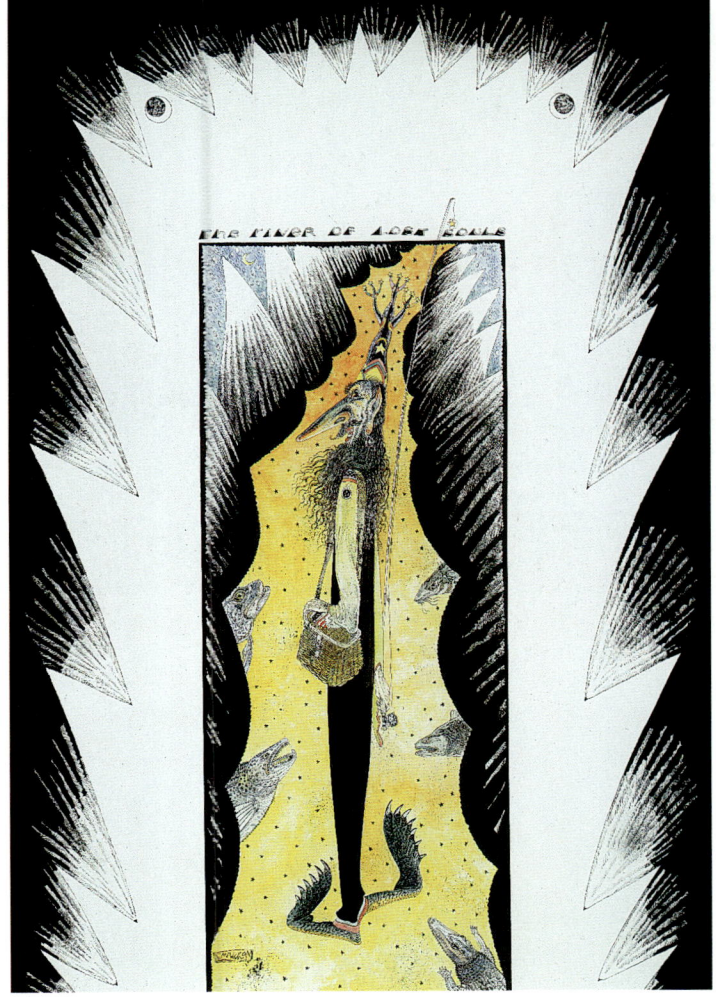

386

387

388

Artist: **JOHN P. MAGGARD III**

Art Director: William Hillenbrand

Client: Building Profit

Medium: Acrylic, oil on Strathmore

Size: 14" x 10 1/2"

389

Artist: **C. F. PAYNE**

Art Director: Ben Ross

Client: Art Directors Club of Cincinnati

Medium: Mixed on board

Size: 14" x 25"

390

Artist: **MICHAEL PARASKEVAS**

Art Directors: Michael Paraskevas
Michele Walton

Client: Bide-A-Wee

Medium: Acrylic on canvas

Size: 40" x 30"

391

Artist: **JOHN PATRICK**

Art Director: John Patrick

Client: Scott Hull Assoc.

Medium: Mixed

Size: 15 1/2" x 12"

388

389

390

391

392
Artist: **FRED OTNES**
Art Director: John deCesare
Client: Reece Galleries
Medium: Mixed, collage on linen
Size: 26" x 21"

393
Artist: **MICHAEL PARASKEVAS**
Art Directors: Michael Paraskevas
Julie Fitzgerald
Client: Southampton Hospital
Medium: Acrylic on board
Size: 28" x 33"

394
Artist: **THEO RUDNAK**
Art Director: Dennis Michael Dimos
Client: U.S. Facilities Corp.
Medium: Gouache on cotton
Strathmore
Size: 14" x 10"

395
Artist: **THEO RUDNAK**
Art Director: Craig Butler
Client: The Workbook
Medium: Gouache on cotton
Strathmore
Size: 15 1/2" x 13 1/2"

396
Artist: **BURT SILVERMAN**
Art Director: Avery Russell
Client: Carnegie Corp.
Medium: Oil on paper
Size: 6" x 9 1/2"

392

393

394

395

396

397

Artist: **ELWOOD H. SMITH**

Art Director: Paul Huber

Agency: Miller Kadanoff

Client: General Motors/Saturn

Medium: Watercolor, ink on water color paper

Size: 17" x 15 1/2"

398

Artist: **JOHN ENGLISH**

Art Director: John English

Client: The Tavern and Top Deck

Medium: Oil on canvas

Size: 24" x 36"

399

Artist: **DUGALD STERMER**

Art Director: Kit Hinrichs

Client: Monterey Bay Aquarium

Medium: Pencil, watercolor on paper

Size: 12" x 28 1/2"

400

Artist: **JOZEF SUMICHRAST**

Art Director: Robert Pearlman

Client: Hadassah

Medium: Watercolor

Size: 22" x 16"

401

Artist: **DUGALD STERMER**

Art Director: Leslee Avchen

Client: Woof Productions

Medium: Pencil, watercolor on paper

Size: 19 1/2" x 15"

397

398

399

400

401

402
Artist: **JOHN THOMPSON**
Client: New Jersey State Council on the Arts
Medium: Acrylic on wood
Size: 19" x 18"

403
Artist: **TIM SPRANSY**
Art Directors: Elizabeth Siegfried
Jim Wilson
Matt Zumbo
Client: P.M.S.
Medium: Mixed
Size: 11" x 8 1/2"

404
Artist: **ROBERT M. SULLIVAN**
Art Director: Kip Bedell
Client: Bedell Cellars
Medium: Acrylic on board
Size: 10 1/2" x 7"

405
Artist: **DAN YACCARINO**
Art Director: Susan R. Hohl
Medium: Goucahe on watercolor paper
Size: 8" x 10 1/2"

402

INSTITUTIONAL
Illustrators 37

403

404

405

406
Artist: **ROBERT GIUSTI**
Art Director: Gail Gonzales
Client: Monterey Bay Aquarium
Medium: Acrylic on linen
Size: 20" x 17"

407
Artist: **CARLOS TORRES**
Medium: Acrylic on board
Size: 16" x 12"

408
Artist: **STEPHEN MAGSIG**
Medium: Oil on linen
Size: 29 1/2" x 23 1/2"

409
Artist: **ROCCO BAVIERA**
Art Director: Laura A. Praiss
Agency: Dorritie Lyons & Nickel, Inc.
Client: Pfizer Inc.
Medium: Mixed assemblage on masonite

406

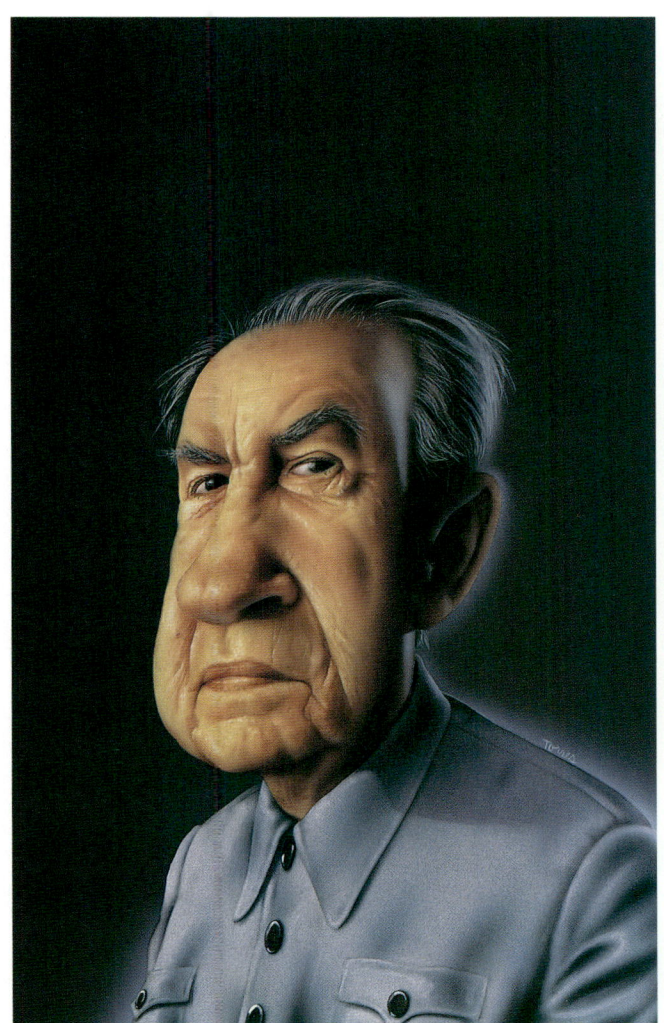
407

408

409

410
Artist: **MICHAEL PLANK**
Art Director: Paul Barker
Client: Hallmark Cards
Medium: Gouache on board
Size: 15" x 21"

411
Artist: **DAVID ROSE**
Art Directors: Anthony Fortuno
Greg Davy
Client: Los Angeles County Transportation Authority
Medium: Ink, charcoal on board
Size: 10" x 15"

412
Artist: **FRED OTNES**
Art Director: Oswaldo Miranda
Client: Grafica Magazine
Medium: Mixed, collage on linen
Size: 17 1/2" x 18"

413
Artist: **ANTHONY BACON VENTI**
Art Director: Bruce Brown
Client: Maine Coast Artists
Medium: Oil on Belgian linen
Size: 40" x 30"

414
Artist: **JAMES STEINBERG**
Art Director: Noreen Doherty
Agency: Hill Holiday
Client: John Hancock
Medium: Gouache on Arches
Size: 11 1/2" x 8"

410

411

INSTITUTIONAL
Illustrators 37

412

413

414

415

Artist: **PHILIPPE WEISBECKER**

Art Director: Lynn Hernandez

Client: Port of Seattle Communication

Medium: Mixed

Size: 16" x 12 1/2"

416

Artist: **FRED OTNES**

Art Director: Oswaldo Miranda

Client: Grafica Magazine

Medium: Mixed, on linen

Size: 16" x 20"

417

Artist: **GREG TUCKER**

Art Director: Rick Vaughn

Agency: Vaughn/Wedeen Creative

Client: Beckett Paper Co.

Medium: Pastel on paper

Size: 22 1/2" x 15 1/2"

418

Artist: **DENNIS ZIEMIENSKI**

Art Director: Fred Parker

Client: Friends of the Sebastiani Theater

Medium: Acrylic on canvas

Size: 47" x 29"

415

416

417

418

419

Artist: **RICHARD LEECH**
Art Director: Howard E. Paine
Client: U.S. Postal Service
Medium: Acrylic
Size: 6" x 9"

420

Artist: **RICHARD LEECH**
Art Director: Howard E. Paine
Client: U.S. Postal Service
Medium: Acrylic
Size: 6" x 9"

421

Artist: **AL HIRSCHFELD**
Art Director: Howard E. Paine
Client: U.S. Postal Service
Medium: Ink
Size: 10" x 6"

422

Artist: **AL HIRSCHFELD**
Art Director: Howard E. Paine
Client: U.S. Postal Service
Medium: Ink
Size: 10" x 6"

423

Artist: **CYNTHIA VON BUHLER**
Art Director: Fritz Klaetke
Medium: Gouache, mixed on canvas
Size: 27" x 27"

419

420

421

422

423

424
Artists: **CHERYL GRIESBACH
STANLEY MARTUCCI**
Art Director: Michael Farmer
Client: American Showcase
Medium: Oil on gessoed masonite
Size: 16 1/2" x 12"

425
Artist: **ETIENNE DELESSERT**
Art Director: Rita Marshall
Client: Society of Illustrators
Medium: Watercolor, pencil on paper
Size: 16" x 11 1/2"

426
Artist: **BILL NELSON**
Art Director: Bill Nelson
Client: Richard Solomon Artists Representative
Medium: Colored pencil on matt board
Size: 13" x 9 1/2"

427
Artist: **JOHN COLLIER**
Art Directors: Wendy Batteau
Louise Fili
Client: Macmillan Inc.
Medium: Pastel on paper
Size: 15" x 15"

INSTITUTIONAL
Illustrators 37

425

426

427

428

Artist: **LINDA HELTON**
Art Director: Linda Helton
Client: Federal Reserve Bank of Dallas
Medium: Acrylic on board
Size: 11" x 17"

429

Artist: **BILL MAYER**
Art Director: David Bartels
Agency: Bartels & Co.
Client: Waxdeck Birdcalling Contest
Medium: Airbrush on board
Size: 14 1/2" x 15 1/2"

430

Artist: **MARK McMAHON**
Art Directors: Tom Reed
Dawn Reed
Client: Reed Interior Design
Medium: Pencil on watercolor paper
Size: 22 1/2" x 30"

431

Artist: **MARK McMAHON**
Art Directors: Tom Reed
Dawn Reed
Client: Reed Interior Design
Medium: Pencil on watercolor paper
Size: 22 1/2" x 30"

428

429

430

431

432

Artist: **JOHN COLLIER**

Art Directors: Wendy Batteau
Louise Fili

Client: Macmillan Inc.

Medium: Pastel on paper

Size: 27 1/2" x 22"

433

Artist: **JOHN COLLIER**

Art Directors: Wendy Batteau
Louise Fili

Client: Macmillan Inc.

Medium: Pastel on paper

Size: 16 1/2" x 16 1/2"

434

Artist: **ERIC BOWMAN**

Medium: Mixed, airbrush on Strathmore Bristol

Size: 9" x 7"

435

Artist: **JOHN P. MAGGARD III**

Art Directors: Scott Hull
Frank Sturgis

Client: Scott Hull Assoc.

Medium: Acrylic, oil on Strathmore

Size: 22 1/2" x 15"

432

INSTITUTIONAL
Illustrators 37

433

434

435

436
Artist: **GUY BILLOUT**
Art Director: Chris Passehl
Client: Orion Capital Corp.
Medium: Watercolor on Bristol vellum
Size: 10 1/4" x 10 1/4"

437
Artist: **BERNIE FUCHS**
Art Director: Ron Maser
Client: Maser Galleries
Medium: Oil on canvas
Size: 34" x 50"

438
Artist: **MARK ENGLISH**
Art Director: Bruce Hartman
Client: Johnson County Cultural Center
Medium: Oil, pastel on paper
Size: 21 1/2" x 18"

439
Artist: **TED COCONIS**
Art Director: Kimio Honda
Agency: DNP America, Inc.
Client: Shoji Matsuzaki
Medium: Oil on canvas
Size: 36 1/2" x 29 1/2"

436

INSTITUTIONAL
Illustrators 37

437

438

439

INTERNATIONAL

JURY

ROCCO CALLARI
United Nations Postal Administration

ETIENNE DELESSERT
Illustrator

TERESA FASOLINO
Illustrator

RAFAL OLBINSKI
Illustrator

SHINICHIRO TORA
Art Director, Popular Photography

440

Artist: **WAYNE ANDERSON**

Art Director: Roger Priddy

Client: Dorling Kindersley

Medium: Crayon & Pencil

Size: 36cm x 21cm

441
Artist: **TAKASHI AKIYAMA**
Art Director: Takashi Akiyama
Client: Pinpoint Gallery
Medium: Serigraphy
Size: 515cm x 364cm

442
Artist: **WAYNE ANDERSON**
Art Director: Wayne Anderson
Client: Wizart
Medium: Crayon & Pencil
Size: 24cm x 18cm

443
Artist: **JERKER ERIKSSON**
Art Director: Peder Schack
Client: Telia
Medium: Watercolor
Size: 36cm x 50cm

441

442

443

444

Artist: **DENNIS BUDGEN**

Art Director: Dr. David A. Eberth

Client: Royal Tyrrell Museum of Palaeontology

Medium: Ink & Watercolor

Size: 39cm x 42cm

445

Artist: **DENNIS BUDGEN**

Art Director: Dr. David A. Eberth

Client: Royal Tyrrell Museum of Palaeontology

Medium: Ink & Watercolor

Size: 39cm x 42cm

446

Artist: **MARCO BOSI**

Art Director: Patrizia Zerbi

Client: Carthusia Edizioni Srl

Medium: Gouache

Size: 36cm x 64cm

447

Artist: **MARCO BOSI**

Art Director: Patrizia Zerbi

Client: Carthusia Edizioni Srl

Medium: Alkyd

Size: 45cm x 64cm

444

445

446

447

448

Artist: **PAUL CAMPION**
Art Director: Dan
Client: Revolver Music Ltd.
Medium: Acrylic & Airbrush
Size: 59cm x 39cm

449

Artist: **HISAO KAWADA**
Art Director: Akira Murakami
Client: Toppan Printing Co., Ltd.
Size: 51.5cm x 36.5cm

450

Artist: **PAOLO D'ALTAN**
Art Director: Lorenzo Marini
Client: Codacons
Medium: Acrylic
Size: 49.5cm x 34cm

451

Artist: **COSA DHERS**
Art Director: Jan Dekker
Client: Organon
Medium: Oil
Size: 116cm x 89cm

449

450

451

452
Artist: **SHINSAKU FUJITA**
Client: Bungeishunju
Size: 28cm x 42cm

453
Artist: **TADAO FURUTA**
Art Director: Madoka Fujinami
Client: Suruga Co., Ltd.
Size: 25cm x 18cm

454
Artist: **JUNICHI ICHIMURA**

455
Artist: **TADAO FURUTA**
Art Director: Taiji Tsukahara
Client: Daiwa-Syoken
Size: 42cm x 59cm

452

453

454

455

456

Artist: **TATSURO KIUCHI**

Art Director: Yumiko Sakuma

Client: Fuzambo

Medium: Oil

Size: 45cm x 50

457

Artist: **TATSURO KIUCHI**

Art Director: Yumiko Sakuma

Client: Fuzambo

Medium: Oil

Size: 45cm x 50cm

458

Artist: **RENE MILOT**

Art Director: Dominique Tessier

Client: Canadair, Fire Prevention

Medium: Oil

Size: 30cm x 56cm

459

Artist: **RENE MILOT**

Art Director: Dominique Tessier

Client: Canadair, Fire Prevention

Medium: Oil

Size: 30cm x 56cm

456

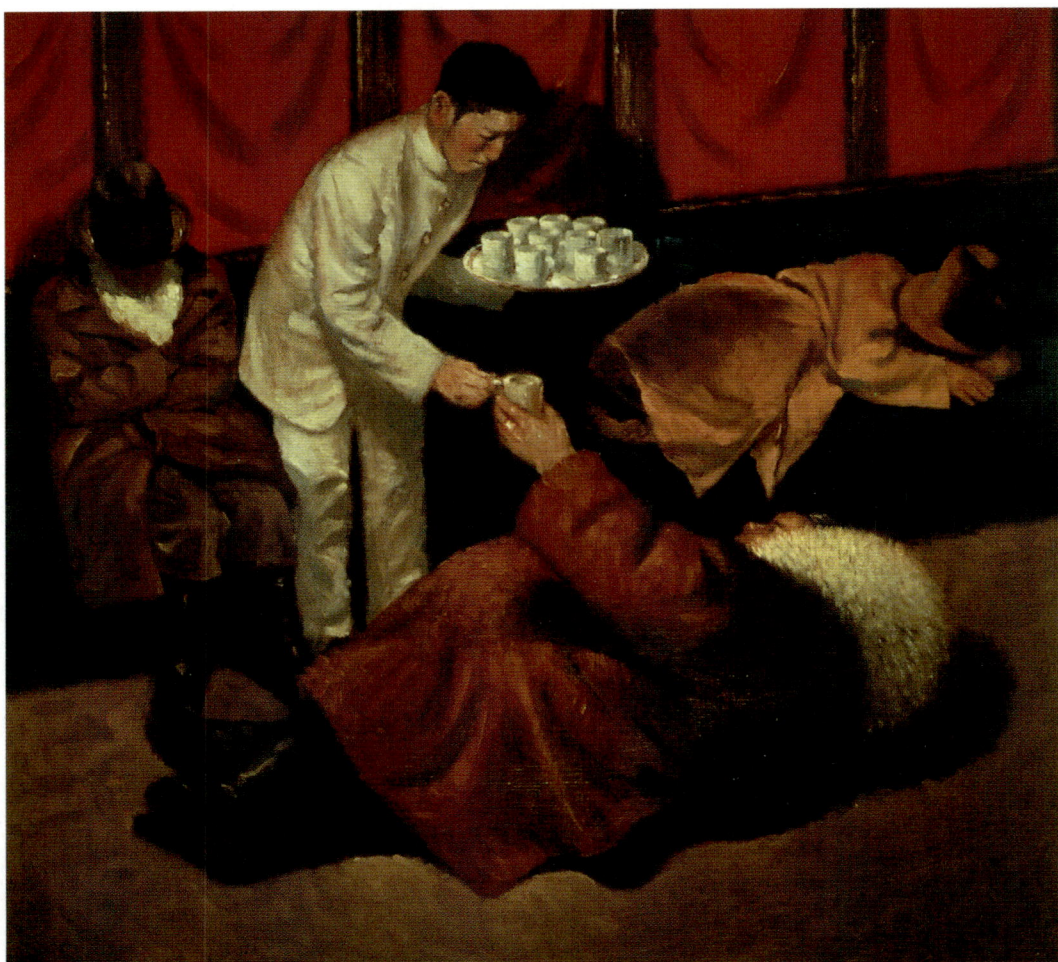

457

458

459

460
Artist: **ALFONS KIEFER**
Medium: Watercolor & Acrylic
Size: 140cm x 100cm

461
Artist: **HENNING LOHLEIN**
Art Director: Robert Crotty
Client: Vnu Publishing
Medium: Acrylic
Size: 42cm x 29cm

462
Artist: **HELMUT LANGEDER**
Art Director: Pierre Roy
Client: PNMD/Publitel
Size: 56cm x 37cm

460

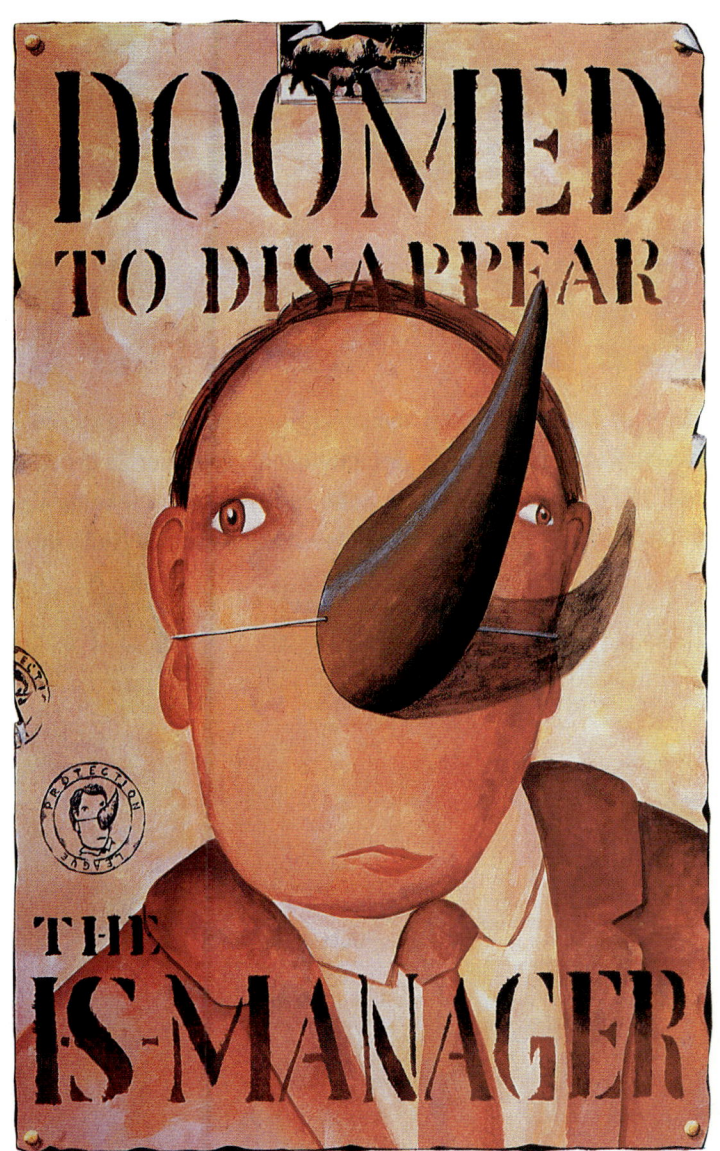

461

462

463

Artist: **RICARDO MARTINEZ**

Art Director: Carmelo Caderot

Client: El Mundo

Medium: Scratchboard

Size: 39.5cm x 33.5cm

464

Artist: **HIROYUKI IZUTSU**

Art Director: Issen Okamoto

Client: American Express International

Size: 40.5cm x 30.5cm

465

Artist: **RUSS WILLMS**

Client: Homecare Magazine

Medium: Watercolor

466

Artist: **HITOSHI MIURA**

Art Director: Hitoshi Miura

Client: JAGDA

Size: 73cm x 103cm

463

INTERNATIONAL
Illustrators 37

464

465

466

467

Artist: **TONO BENAVIDES**

Art Director: Carmelo Caderot

Client: El Mundo

Medium: Oil-Pastel

Size: 47cm x 40cm

468

Artist: **TOMAS LINDELL**

Art Director: John Bark

Client: Moderna Tider

Medium: Acrylic

Size: 20cm x 20cm

469

Artist: **CARLOS NINE**

Art Director: Marc Morgan

Client: Katharine Hamnett

Medium: Watercolor

Size: 37cm x 27cm

470

Artist: **CARLOS NINE**

Art Director: Marc Morgan

Client: Katharine Hamnett

Medium: Watercolor

Size: 37cm x 27cm

467

468

469

470

471
Artist: **THOMAS POSTHUMA**
Art Director: Thomas Posthuma
Client: Typo's en Litho's
Size: 30cm x 50cm

472
Artist: **TREVOR RUTH**
Art Director: Steve Thomas
Client: Australian News Print Mills
Size: 40cm x 40cm

473
Artist: **GARY TAXALI**
Client: The Carrot Gallery
Medium: Alkyd
Size: 45cm x 65cm

471

472

473

474

Artist: **GORO SASAKI**

Art Director: Goro Sasaki

Client: Art Gallery Maya

Medium: Watercolor

Size: 60cm x 35cm

475

Artist: **GORO SASAKI**

Client: Mitsui Insurance Co., Ltd.

Medium: Watercolor

Size: 25cm x 35cm

476

Artist: **GORO SASAKI**

Art Director: Goro Sasaki

Client: Art Gallery Maya

Medium: Watercolor

Size: 50cm x 32cm

474

475

476

477
Artist: **HISAKO NAKAYAMA**
Size: 720cm x 925cm

478
Artist: **HISAKO NAKAYAMA**
Size: 720cm x 925cm

479
Artist: **P. J. LYNCH**
Art Director: Amelia Edwards
Client: Walker Books/ Candlewick Press
Medium: Watercolor & Gouache
Size: 37cm x 49cm

480
Artist: **HISAKO NAKAYAMA**
Size: 920cm x 1170cm

477

478

479

480

481
Artist: **JOSEPH SALINA**
Art Director: Steve Manley
Client: Cottage Life
Medium: Acrylic
Size: 27cm x 21cm

482
Artist: **JOSEPH SALINA**
Art Director: Susan Meingast
Client: Homemakers Magazine
Medium: Acrylic
Size: 19cm x 29cm

483
Artist: **TAKASHI OHNO**
Art Director: Masataka Saito
Client: Achilles
Medium: Acrylic
Size: 58cm x 79cm

481

INTERNATIONAL
Illustrators 37

482

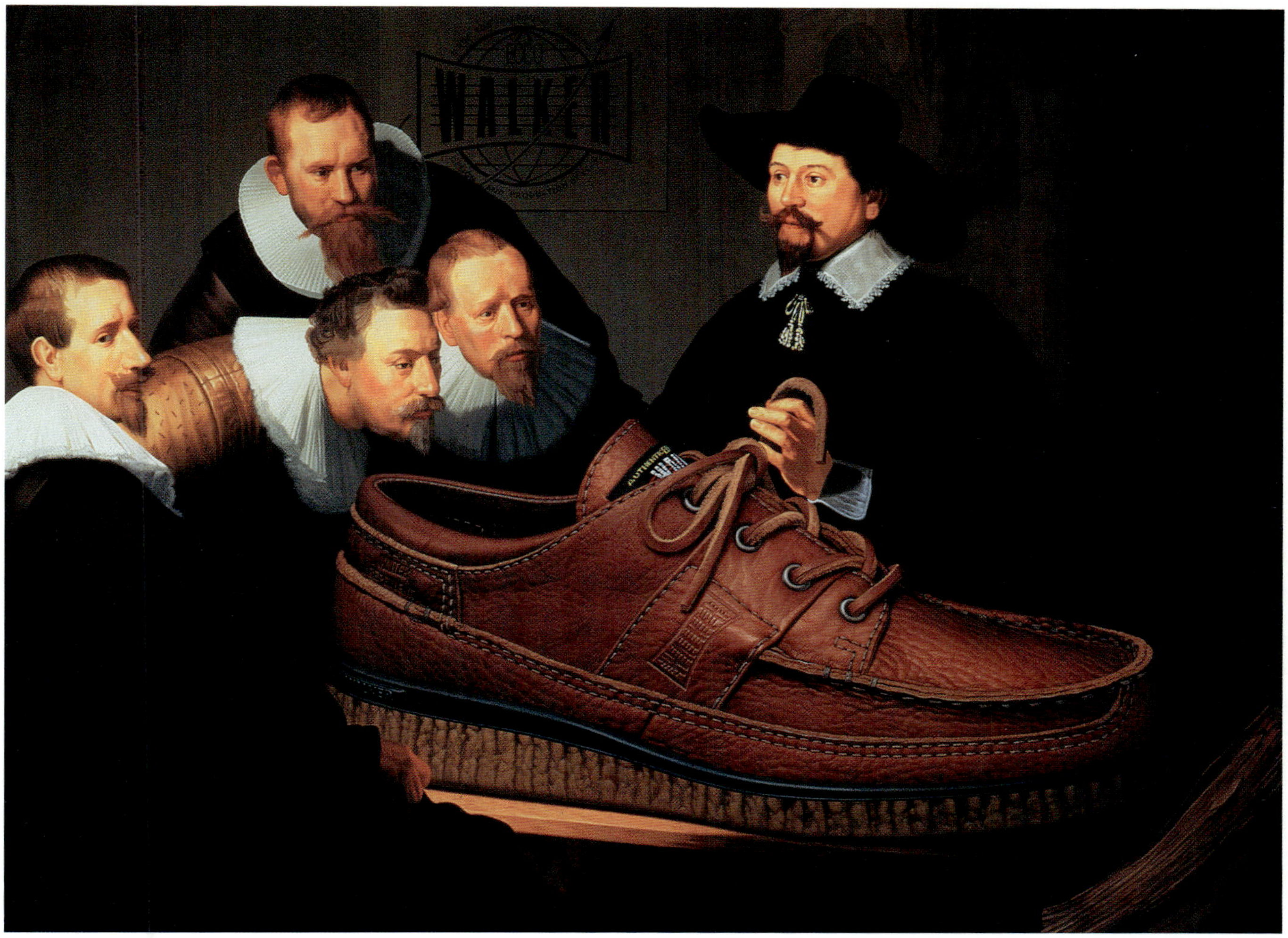

483

484

Artist: **YASUTAKA TAGA**

Art Director: Yusuke Matsuoka

Client: Takarajimasha, Inc.

Medium: 3-D Illustration of Clay, Acrylic & Computer

Size: 40cm x 30cm

485

Artist: **YASUTAKA TAGA**

Art Director: Yasutaka Taga

Client: Kitanihon Broadcasting Co., Ltd.

Medium: 3-D Illustration of Clay, Acrylic & Computer

Size: 40cm x 30cm

486

Artist: **YASUTAKA TAGA**

Art Director: Yusuke Matsuoka

Client: Takarajimasha, Inc.

Medium: 3-D Illustration of Clay, Acrylic & Computer

Size: 40cm x 30cm

487

Artist: **FLETCHER SIBTHORP**

Art Director: Sue Turner

Client: British Telecom

Medium: Oil

Size: 90cm x 60cm

485

486

487

488
Artist: **RENE MILOT**
Art Director: Gord Smith
Client: Tafelmusik
Medium: Oil
Size: 96cm x 69cm

489
Artist: **SHUN-ICHI SEKI**
Medium: Acrylic
Size: 60.5cm x 91cm

490
Artist: **CARLOS NINE**
Art Director: J. Binzstock
Client: Sevil Deu Nosse
Medium: Watercolor
Size: 30cm x 23cm

491
Artist: **RUSS WILLMS**
Art Director: Russ Willms
Client: Priority Man
Medium: Watercolor

488

489

490

491

492
Artist: **JANET WOOLLEY**
Art Director: Ronnie Fairweather
Client: Penguin Group
Size: 57cm x 39cm

493
Artist: **FUMIO WATANABE**
Art Director: Miwa Tanaka
Client: Meiji Seimei Co.
Size: 58.5cm x 43cm

494
Artist: **BEN TOMITA**
Art Director: Koichi Matsushita
Client: KDD Co., Ltd.
Size: 40cm x 45cm

NEW VISIONS

The Society of Illustrators is once again proud to reproduce the catalogue of its Annual Student Scholarship Competition in this year's Annual Book so that you may see illustration from the perspective of these talented young artists.

Over 5,000 entries were received from 100 accredited institutions nationwide, from which 118 works by young artists were selected by a prestigious jury. Everett Davidson was instrumental in the crucial fund raising for awards and Alvin Pimsler, Chairman of the Education Committee, once again guided the jury through the lengthy selection process. The original works were exhibited at the Society of Illustrators Museum of American Illustration.

We are grateful to the many individuals, foundations, and organizations who contribute to the Scholarship Fund each year; their generous gifts support the bright futures of these worthy students. Contributors are listed in the following pages of "New Visions."

Exceptional craftsmanship and a high level of conceptual excitement are boldly present in the works of the young artists catalogued here. It is not difficult to imagine students from across the country entering the marketplace with the tools necessary to achieve success.

NEW VISIONS

PRESIDENT'S MESSAGE

Sincere congratulations to the select few chosen for the Society's 1995 Student Scholarship Competition. Accept this recognition by a jury of professionals as your first step on the long, arduous journey towards your career as an illustrator.

I applaud the teachers, chairs and institutions represented this year. You, too, have risen above stern competition. The efforts you put into preparation, assignment, critique, studio and class instruction are rewarded by the development you see here in your students.

The Society of Illustrators is fortunate to have a superior cadre of dedicated volunteers to make this competition happen. My personal thanks are extended to Al Pimsler, the Chairman of the Education Committee and his committee which did an "above and beyond" job this year. Also contributing a superior job this year was Everett Davidson who chaired the Annual Christmas Auction, the major fund raiser for all the Society's scholarships.

Sponsorship of awards continues to be a satisfying "two way street" for both donors and recipients...giving back to the industry and continuing the memories of loved ones. The Society expresses its appreciation to: The Starr Foundation, The Reader's Digest Association, Jellybean Photographics, The Norman Rockwell Museum at Stockbridge, The Franklin Mint Foundation for the Arts, Norma and Alvin Pimsler and the friends and families of Albert Dorne, Pearl Dugas, Herman Lambert, Augie Napoli, Frances Means, Harry Rosenbaum and Meg Wohlberg.

1995 marks the 15th year of the primary sponsorship of this competition by Hallmark Cards of Kansas City, Missouri. Their matching grants share the students success with their institutions. Their support makes this catalogue and its distribution possible. The Society thanks all at Hallmark.

Peter Fiore
President

CHAIRMAN'S MESSAGE

The 20 jurors, all professionals in the field of illustration, worked long and hard selecting the artwork that appears in this show. They viewed over 5,000 slides submitted by students from art schools and colleges all across the United States, and, from that number, chose 118 pieces of art to be shown.

My congratulations to you who have withstood the test of submitting, being judged and selected. You are a very select group indeed.

Your parents, who were supportive and encouraged your efforts and vision, and the instructors, who are helping you to achieve your goals, are to be commended as well.

The future of illustration is in good hands to continue its exciting and long history as part of our culture.

Alvin J. Pimsler
Chairman,
Education Committee

ACKNOWLEDGEMENTS

COMMITTEE:
Alvin J. Pimsler, Chair;
James Barkley, Steve Cieslawski,
Jacques Parker, Jon Weiman,
Everett Davidson, Chair,
Annual Christmas Auction

JURY:
Al Cetta, Ariane Dewey, Linda Fennimore,
Barbara Garrison, Donato Giancola,
Ned Glattauer, Carl Hantman, Diane Luger,
Patrick Milbourn, Dale Moyer, Jacques Parker,
Steve Parton, Barnett Plotkin, Stan Popko,
Jan Pyk, Ed Renfro, Hodges Soileau,
George Thompson, Anne Twomey,
Bob Ziering

HALLMARK CORPORATE FOUNDATION

Hallmark Corporate Foundation Matching Grants

The Hallmark Corporate Foundation of Kansas City, Missouri, is again this year supplying full matching grants for all of the awards in the Society's Student Scholarship Competition. Grants, restricted to the Illustration Departments, are awarded to the following institutions:

9,450	School of Visual Arts
3,600	University of the Arts
2,350	Art Center College of Design
1,600	Academy of Art College
1,500	University of Arizona
1,500	Kansas City Art Institute
1,500	New World School of the Arts
1.500	Ringling School of Art and Design
1.500	Syracuse University
1,500	Utah State University
1,200	Fashion Institute of Technology
1,000	California State University at Fullerton
1,000	duCret School of the Arts
1,000	Virginia Commonwealth University
500	Paier College of Art
450	Kendall College of Art & Design
250	Columbus College of Art & Design
200	Maryland Institute, College of Art
200	Massachusetts College of Art
200	University of Massachusetts at Dartmouth

THE AWARDS

Dana Duane Craft
Richard Romeo, Instructor
New World School of the Arts
$1500 Dick Blick Art Materials Award

Kyle Margiotta
Mark Tocchet, Instructor
University of the Arts
$2000 Robert H. Blattner Award

Gennaro Capasso
Marvin Mattelson, Instructor
School of Visual Arts
$1500 Jellybean Photographics Award

Alex Leon
Sam Martine, Instructor
School of Visual Arts
$2000 Albert Dorne Award

Jason Rich
Glen Edwards, Instructor
Utah State University
$1500 The Norman Rockwell Museum at Stockbridge Award

THE AWARDS

Huy Meng Lov
Robert Rodriguez, Instructor
Art Center College of Design
$1500 The Reader's Digest Association Award

Rick O'Brien
Jerold Bishop, Instructor
University of Arizona
$1500 Franklin Mint Foundation for the Arts Award

Wayne Wilkes
Steve Mayse, Instructor
Kansas City Art Institute
$1500 The Starr Foundation Award

Todd R. Reinhart
Bob Dacey, Instructor
Syracuse University
$1500 The Reader's Digest Association Award

Agnes Legowiecka
Max Ginsburg, Instructor
School of Visual Arts
$1500 Jellybean Photographics Award

THE AWARDS

Kathy W. Kim
Larry Johnson, Instructor
California State University at Fullerton
$1000 Franklin Mint Foundation
for the Arts Award

Jin H. Chung
Alex Bostic, Instructor
Virginia Commonwealth
University
$1000
The Norman Rockwell
Museum at Stockbridge
Award

Andrew F. Engel
Brian Townsend, Instructor
duCret School of the Arts
$1000 Barbara Carr Award
in Memory of Her Mother,
Pearl F. Rounds Carr Dugas

Rudy Speerschneider
Regan Dunnick, Instructor
Ringling School of Art and Design
$1500 The Starr Foundation Award

David Chen
Brad Durham, Instructor
Art Center College of Design
$750 Award in Memory of
Herman Lambert

Donald Sipley
Griesbach/Martucci, Instructors
School of Visual Arts
$1000 Norma and Alvin Pimsler Award

Madeleine Hope Arthurs
Sam Martine, Instructor
School of Visual Arts
$750 Award in Memory of
Augie Napoli

THE AWARDS

Carly Delong
Graham Chaffee, Instructor
Academy of Art College
$750 Kirchoff/Wohlberg Award in Memory of Frances Means

Jiyeon Lee
Paul Kratter, Instructor; Academy of Art College
$750 Award in Memory of Harry Rosenbaum

Patrick Carney
Marvin Mattelson, Instructor
School of Visual Arts
$500 The Starr Foundation Award

Mark Mascolo
Peter Fiore, Instructor
School of Visual Arts
$750 Award in Memory of Meg Wohlberg

Megan Berkheiser
Ralph Giguere/Bryn Barnard, Instructors
University of the Arts
$500 The Starr Foundation Award

Alison Mennor
Renee Foulks/Larry Donahue, Instructors
University of the Arts
$750 Friends of the Institute of
Commercial Art Award

THE AWARDS

Gina Matarazzo
Ralph Giguere, Instructor
University of the Arts
$250 Award

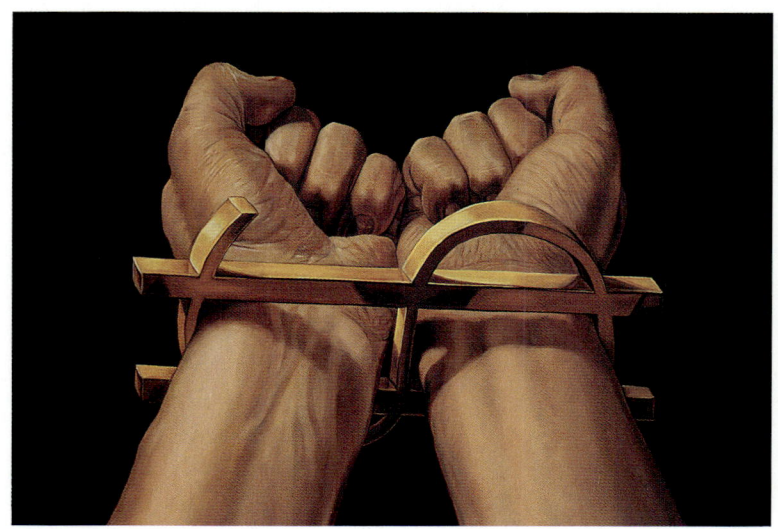

John Schieffer III
Tim O'Brien, Instructor
Paier College of Art
$500 The Starr Foundation Award

Tony Curanaj
Marvin Mattelson, Instructor
School of Visual Arts
$500 Albert Dorne Award

Beth Bojarski
Jon McDonald, Instructor
Kendall College of Art & Design
$250 Award

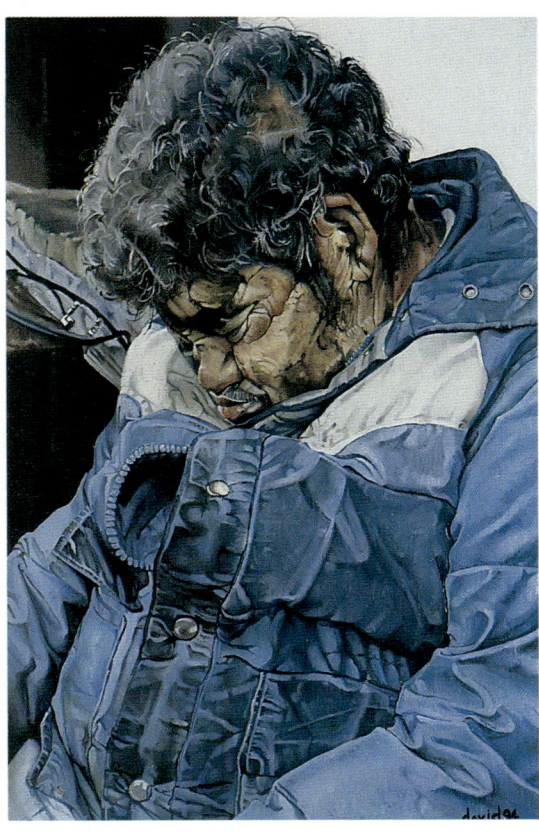

David Lee
Herbert Tauss, Instructor
Fashion Institute of Technology
$500 Albert Dorne Award

Den Phok
Kam Mak, Instructor
Fashion Institute of Technology
$500 The Starr Foundation Award

THE AWARDS

Alex B. McDaniel
Steve Botts, Instructor
Columbus College of Art & Design
$250 Award

Michael Evans
Marvin Mattelson, Instructor
School of Visual Arts
$200 Award

Anna Maria Lalli
Sarah Reader, Instructor
Fashion Institute of Technology
$200 Award

Lori Earley
Marvin Mattelson, Instructor
School of Visual Arts
$200 Award

Timothy Cronin
Jack Potter, Instructor
School of Visual Arts
$250 Award

John Carbone
Irena Roman, Instructor
Massachusetts College of Art
$200 Award

Andrew Barthelmes
Francis Jetter, Instructor
School of Visual Arts
$200 Award

THE AWARDS

Ron Zawistowski
Jon McDonald, Instructor
Kendall College of Art & Design
$200 Award

Eric Schwinn
Vasant Nayak, Instructor
Maryland Institute,
College of Art
$200 Award

Jason Pichon
Robert Barry, Instructor
University of Massachusetts at Dartmouth
$200 Award

Robert Revels
Graham Chaffee, Instructor
Academy of Art College
$100 Award

Mia Bosna
Mark Tocchet, Instructor
University of the Arts
$100 Award

Armand Baltazar
Gary Meyer, Instructor
Art Center College of Design
$100 Award

Sam Emler
Sal Catalano, Instructor
School of Visual Arts
$100 Award

THE EXHIBIT

1. **Bob Abric**
   Jack DeGraffenried, Instructor
   Sacred Heart University

2. **Kristen Bennett**
   Robert Krajecki, Instructor
   American Academy of Art

3. **Bruce Bibler**
   Dom Scibilia, Instructor
   Cleveland Institute of Art

4. **Bruce Bibler**
   Nan Wiggins, Instructor
   Cleveland Institute of Art

5. **Mia Bosna**
   Mark Tocchet, Instructor
   University of the Arts

6. **Erika Nelson Bowder**
   Chris Willey, Instructor
   Central Missouri State University

7. **Gennaro Capasso**
   Mark Kaplan, Instructor
   School of Visual Arts

8. **John Carbone**
   Theresa Flavin/Irena Roman, Instructors
   Massachusetts College of Art

9. **Michelle Chang**
   Jeff Decoster, Instructor
   Academy of Art College

10. **Donna Christensen**
    Jon McDonald, Instructor
    Kendall College of Art & Design

11. **Stephen M. Clark**
    Leon Parson, Instructor
    Ricks College

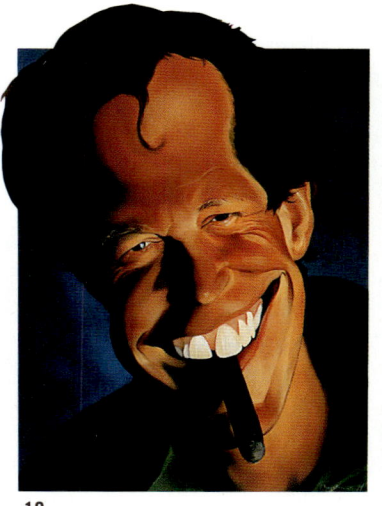
10

2

1

4

5

3

6

8

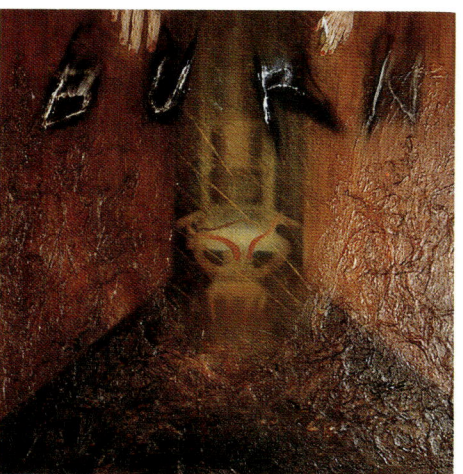
9

11

7

THE EXHIBIT

12   **Marc Contreras**
David Christiana, Instructor
University of Arizona

13   **Mark Covell**
Tim O'Brien, Instructor
Paier College of Art

14   **Tony Curanaj**
MarvinMattelson/Griesbach/Martucci, Instructors
School of Visual Arts

15   **Juan Diaz**
Stanley Martucci, Instructor
School of Visual Arts

16   **Tobin Dorn**
George Pratt, Instructor
Pratt Institute

17   **Chad Dunbar**
Rory Bonnet, Instructor
Rocky Mountain College of Art and Design

18   **Sam Emler**
Sal Catalano, Instructor
School of Visual Arts

19   **Andrew F. Engel**
Kathy DeBlasio, Instructor
duCret School of the Arts

20   **Michael Evans**
Marvin Mattelson, Instructor
School of Visual Arts

21   **Tim Evans**
Estelle Hickman, Instructor
Columbus College of Art & Design

22   **David M. Ferguson**
Bob Dacey, Instructor
Syracuse University

22

13

20

15

21

18

14

19

16

17

12

THE EXHIBIT

23 **Nathan Fowkes**
Bob Kato, Instructor
Art Center College of Design

24 **Nathan Fowkes**
Richard Bankall, Instructor
Art Center College of Design

25 **Nathan Fox**
Brent Watkinson, Instructor
Kansas City Art Institute

26 **Chris Gennaro**
Gregory Crane, Instructor
School of Visual Arts

27 **Michel Gibbs**
Gerry Contreras, Instructor
Pratt Institute

28 **Peter Gremett**
Courtney Granner, Instructor
San Jose State University

29 **Amy J. Grigg**
Tim O'Brien, Instructor
Paier College of Art

30 **John Phillip Hart**
Leon Parson, Instructor
Ricks College

31 **John Hermanowski, Jr.**
Jack Endewelt, Instructor
School of Visual Arts

32 **Ronda Hoelzer**
Morton Kaish, Instructor
Fashion Institute of Technology

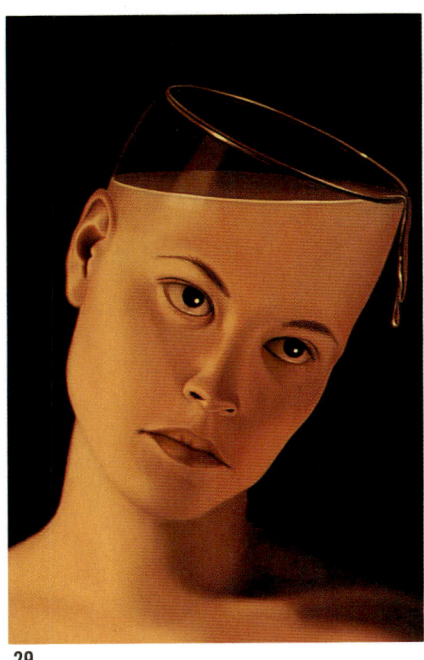
29

24

25

28

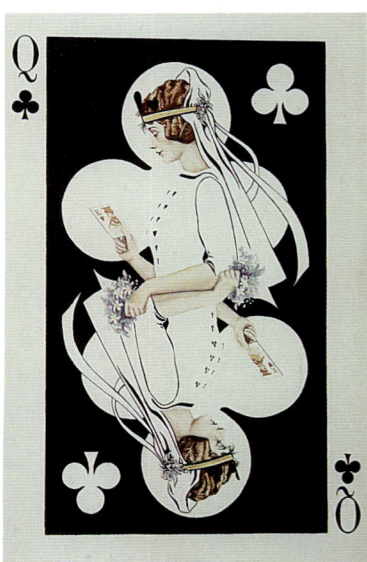
30

27

32

23

31

26

THE EXHIBIT

33 **Gordon James**
Julie Lieberman, Instructor
School of Visual Arts

34 **Evan Jenkins**
Bruce Sharp, Instructor
Art Institute of Seattle

35 **Robb Jones**
Rory Bonnet, Instructor
Rocky Mountain College of
Art and Design

36 **Anthony Karlic**
Jim Bennett, Instructor
School of Visual Arts

37 **Roseld Laguatan**
Courtney Granner, Instructor
San Jose State University

38 **Michael Lancellotti**
Marvin Mattelson, Instructor
School of Visual Arts

39 **Michael Lancellotti**
Marvin Mattelson, Instructor
School of Visual Arts

40 **Michaux Land**
Marie Weaver, Instructor
University of Alabama at Birmingham

41 **Tammy LaValla**
Bob Dacey, Instructor
Syracuse University

42 **David Lee**
Morton Kaish, Instructor
Fashion Institute of Technology

36

42

41

33

40

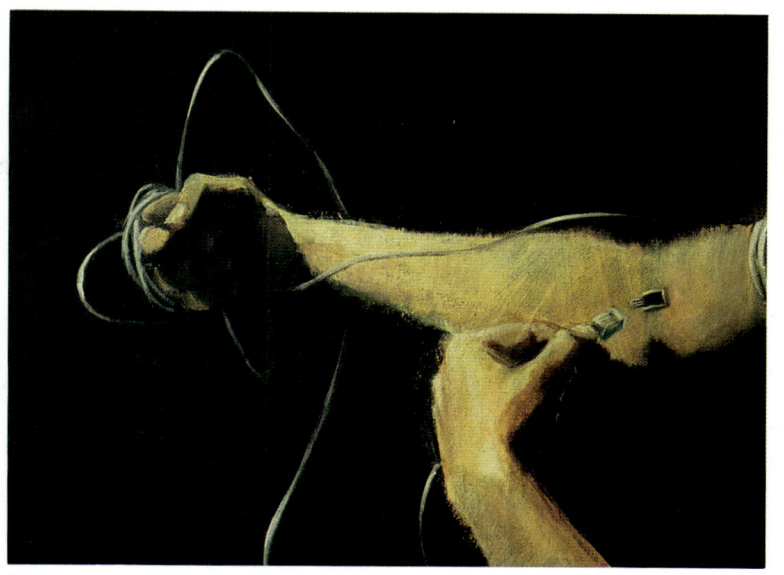
37

34

35

39

38

THE EXHIBIT

43 **Anna Leong**
Dwight Harmon, Instructor
Art Center College of Design

44 **PJ Loughran**
Wendy Popp, Instructor
Parsons School of Design

45 **Huy Meng Lov**
Jon Conrad, Instructor
Art Center College of Design

46 **Bill Madigan**
Jack Endewelt, Instructor
School of Visual Arts

47 **Shannon Maer**
Marvin Mattelson, Instructor
School of Visual Arts

48 **Stan J. Makowski**
Regan Dunnick, Instructor
Ringling School of Art and Design

49 **Steven S. Martinez**
Teresa Fasolino, Instructor
School of Visual Arts

50 **Elizabeth Mates**
Jack Endewelt, Instructor
School of Visual Arts

51 **Aubry McClure**
Leon Parson, Instructor
Ricks College

52 **Alex B. McDaniel**
John Kortlander, Instructor
Columbus College of Art & Design

53 **George McPherson**
Jim Bennett, Instructor
School of Visual Arts

53

44

51

46

52

49

50

48

47

45

43

THE EXHIBIT

54 **Kadir Nelson**
Gerry Contreras, Instructor
Pratt Institute

55 **Annelies Nieveld**
William Senior, Instructor
duCret School of the Arts

56 **Jennifer Oakley**
Jon McDonald, Instructor
Kendall College of Art & Design

57 **Saunghee Park**
Marvin Mattelson, Instructor
School of Visual Arts

58 **Jason Pichon**
Robert Barry, Instructor
University of Massachusetts at Dartmouth

59 **Heather Reuterdahl**
Jon McDonald, Instructor
Kendall College of Art & Design

60 **Jason Rich**
Glen Edwards, Instructor
Utah State University

61 **Willie Rosas**
Griesbach/Martucci, Instructors
School of Visual Arts

62 **Willie Rosas**
Marvin Mattelson, Instructor
School of Visual Arts

63 **Manveet Saluja**
Sal Catalano, Instructor
School of Visual Arts

64 **David Sean SanAngelo**
Tim O'Brien, Instructor
Paier College of Art

56

61

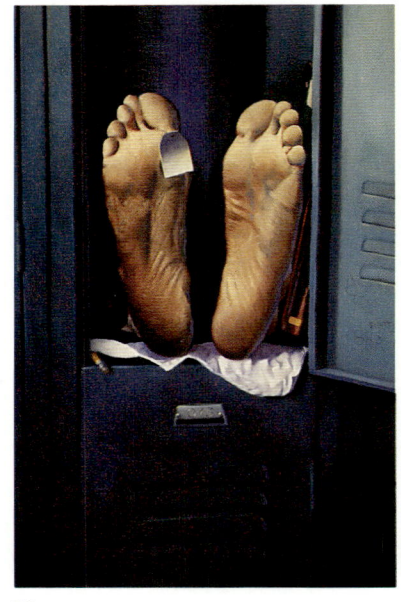
64

54

THE EXHIBIT

65 **Marv Sangsland**
John Kilmaster, Instructor
Boise State University

66 **Anna Santarcangelo**
Joo Chung, Instructor
School of Visual Arts

67 **John Schieffer III**
Tim O'Brien, Instructor
Paier College of Art

68 **Ken Schwartz**
Mark Tocchet, Instructor
University of the Arts

69 **Pak So**
Bob Dorsey, Instructor
Rochester Institute of Technology

70 **Matthew Somma**
Laura Lasworth, Instructor
Art Center College of Design

71 **Julie Sparks**
Chuck Scalin, Instructor
Virginia Commonwealth University

72 **Evan Spiridellis**
Alan Reingold, Instructor
Parsons School of Design

73 **Philip Straub**
Tim O'Brien, Instructor
Paier College of Art

74 **Patrick Timmes**
George Fernandez, Instructor
Long Island University at C.W. Post

75 **Susan J. Wieringa**
Jon McDonald, Instructor
Kendall College of Art & Design
®Hormel Foods Corporation

65

67

73

74

70

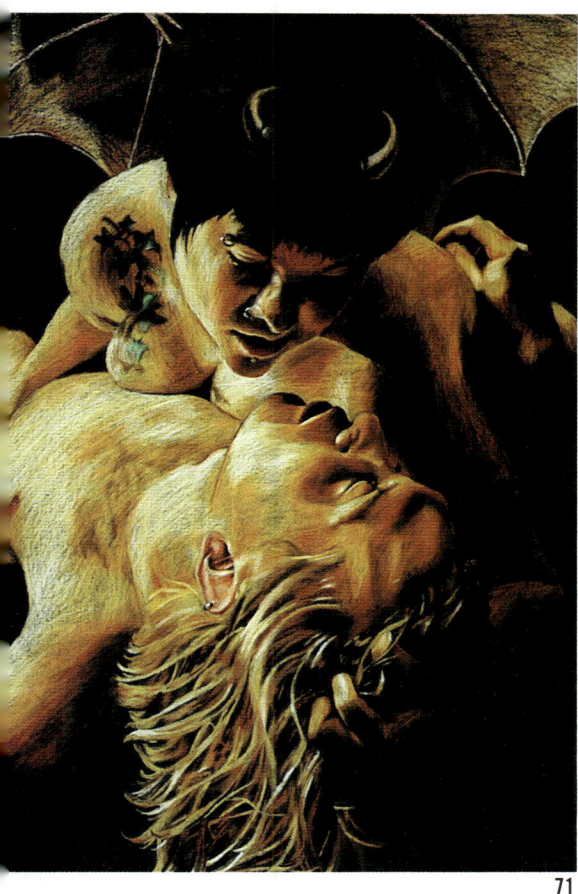

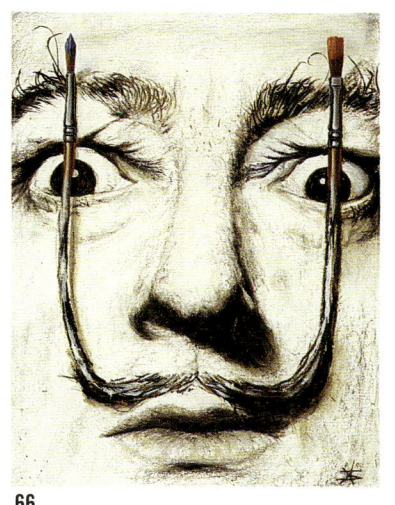

ARTIST INDEX

Adel, Daniel, 142, 197, 234
50 W. 77th St., #PH1
New York, NY 10024
(212) 787-0617

Alder, Kelynn, 12
5 Captain's Walk
Setauket, NY 11733
(516) 246-5874

Allen, Terry, 63
164 Daniel Lau Terrace
Staten Island, NY 10301
(718) 727-0723

Anderson, Paul, 49
182 Christie Ave.
Clifton, NJ 07011
(201) 340-4914

Ang, Thom, 337
1622 1/2 Bank St.
S. Pasadena, CA 91030
(818) 441-0423

Arday, Don, 333
616 Arbor Creek Dr.
DeSoto, TX 75115
(214) 223-6235
Rep: (214) 720-2272

Arisman, Marshall, 8, 11, 44
314 W. 100th St.
New York, NY 10025
(212) 662-2289

Ascencios, N., 15, 72
918 Metropolitan Ave. #1L
Brooklyn, NY 11211
(718) 388-7931

Asmussen, Don, 17, 334
1903 Broderick St. #5
San Francisco, CA 94115
(415) 885-6195

Atkinson, Janet, 183
359 Ovington Ave.
Brooklyn, NY 11209
(718) 836-9335

Baldwin, Christopher, 305
19514 14th Ave.
NE. Seattle, WA 98155
(206) 367-9042
Rep: (206) 282-8558

Balogh, Dennis, 16
8183 Joyce Rd.
Broadview Hts., OH 44147
(216) 546-9223

Barnard, Bryn, 332
432 Point Caution Dr.
Newark Friday Harbor
WA 98250
(306) 378-6355

Bascove, 255
319 50th St. PHH
New York, NY 10022
(212) 888-0038

Baviera, Rocco, 409
41 King William St. #210
Hamilton, Ontario, L8R 1A2
Canada
1-(905) 570-0004
Rep: (310) 826-1332

Beck, Melinda, 264
44 Fourth Pl. #2
Brooklyn, NY 11231
(718) 624-6538

Behm, Kim, 247
1323 W. 2nd St.
Cedar Falls, IA 50613
(319) 277-3197

Bennett, James, 335, 336
Pipersville, PA
(201) 963-1457
Rep: Richard Solomon
(212) 683-1362

Bennett, Thomas, 24
325 Clinton St. #4
Brooklyn, NY 11231
(718) 596-1388

Benny, Mike, 9, 324, 341, 342
2773 Knollwood Dr.
Cameron Park, CA 95682
(916) 677-9142

Billout, Guy, 14, 436
225 Lafayette St. #1008
New York, NY 10012-4015
(212) 431-6350

Blackshear, Thomas, 338
220 Elm Circle
Colorado Springs, CO 80906
(719) 636-5009

Blechman, R.O., 26
2 West 47th St.
New York, NY 10036
(212) 869-1630

Bleck, Linda, 147
642 W. Aldine #1
Chicago, IL 60657
(312) 281-0286

Blitt, Barry, 23
34 Lincoln Ave.
Greenwich, CT 06830
(203) 622-2988

Boatwright, Phil, 43, 100
2342 Stillwater Dr.
Mesquite, TX 75181
(214) 222-7571

Bowers, David, 356
100 Scott Way
Carnegie, PA 15106
(412) 276-7224

Bowman, Eric, 434
11605 S.W. Terra Linda
Beaverton, OR 97005
(503) 644-1016

Bralds, Braldt, 18, 239, 315
13 Herrada Ct.
Santa Fe, NM 87505
(505) 466-3603

Bramhall, William, 31
c/o Riley Illustration
155 W. 15th St.
New York, NY 10011
Rep: (212) 989-8770

Brown, Calef, 128
12761 Caswell Ave.
Los Angeles, CA 90066
(310) 397-7603
Rep: (317) 920-0068

Browne, Anthony, 143, 158
c/o Julia MacRae Books
Rabdom House
20 Vauxhall Bridge Rd.
London SW1 25A, England
011-44-84-3847-202

Burckhardt, Marc, 159
112 West 41st St.
Austin, TX 78751
(512) 474-9781

Burke, Philip, 10, 20, 22
1948 Juron Dr.
Niagara Falls, NY 14304
(716) 297-0345

Busch, Lonnie, 331
15 N. Gore #202
St. Louis, MO 63119
(314) 962-7099
Rep: (212) 889-3337

Carmichael, Cynthia J., 59
7830 Barnsbury
W. Bloomfield, MI 48324
(810) 363-5575

Ciardiello, Joe, 29, 30
2182 Clove Rd.
Staten Island, NY 10305
(718) 727-4757

Clapp, John, 366
4961 Monaco Dr.
Pleasanton, CA 94566
(510) 462-6444

Cober, Alan E., 45, 154, 329,
330, 373
95 Croton Dam Rd.
Ossining, NY 10562
(914) 941-8696

Coconis, Ted, 439
PO Box 758
Cedar Key, FL 32625
(904) 543-5720

Collier, John, 1, 52, 96, 325,
427, 432, 433
Garland, TX
(214) 530-4142
Rep: Richard Solomon
(212) 683-1362

Colon, Raul, 19, 144, 149,
150, 166
43-C Heritage Dr.
New City, NY 10956
(914) 639-1505

Cox, Paul, 249
Norfolk, England
011-44-1-55-382-9313
Rep: Richard Solomon
(212) 683-1362

Craft, Kinuko, 28, 153
83 Litchfield Rd.
Norfolk, CT 06058
(203) 542-5018
Rep: (212) 486-9644

Craig, Daniel, 257, 282
118 E. 26th St. #302
Minneapolis, MN 55404
(612) 871-4539

Crawford, Dale, 321
809 Young Ave.
Chattanooga, TN 37405
(615) 266-5971

Crawford, Robert, 176, 209
123 Minortown Rd.
Woodbury, CT 06798
(203) 266-0059

Cunningham, Robert M., 354
45 Cornwall Rd.
Warren, CT 06754
(203) 868-2702

Curry, Tom, 32, 33, 34, 241
901 W. Sul Ross
Alpine, TX 79830
(915) 837-2311

Davis, Bob A., 35
7992 Parkford St. N.W.
Massillon, OH 44646
(216) 833-6500

Davis, Paul, 92
14 E. 4th St. #504
New York, NY 10012
(212) 420-8789

Day, Rob, 248
6095 Ralston Ave.
Indianapolis, IN 46220
(317) 253-9000

ARTIST INDEX

Dearth, Gregory M., 243, 245, 283, 374
4041 Beal Rd.
Franklin, OH 45005
(513) 746-5970
Rep: (513) 433-8383

Deas, Michael J., 180, 345
39 Sidney Pl.
Brooklyn Heights, NY 11201
(718) 852-5630

DeGrace, John, 240, 246
c/o Shannon/Avery
327 E. 89th St.
New York, NY 10128
Rep: (212) 831-5650

Delessert, Etienne, 155, 156, 178, 244, 326, 425
PO Box 1689
Lakeville, CT 06039
(203) 435-0061

DeSantis, Diana, 251
34 School St.
East Williston, NY 11596
(516) 747-7737

de Sève, Peter, 36, 37, 38, 157
25 Park Pl.
Brooklyn, NY 11217
(718) 398-8099

Dodson, Jeff, 39
3808 Fairway Cr.
Las Vegas, NV 89108
(702) 648-0702

Downs, Richard, 40
24294 Saradella Ct.
Murrieta, CA 92562
(909) 677-3452

Doyle, John Carroll, 242, 250
354 1/2 King St.
Charleston, SC 29401
(803) 723-3269

Drawson, Blair, 42
14 Leuty Ave.
Toronto, Ontario M4E 2R3
Canada
1-(416) 693-7774

Drescher, Henrik, 88, 148, 162, 220
c/o Joe Weber
942 Country Club Dr.
Teaneck, NJ 07666-5600
(201) 833-0813

Dugin, Andrei, 194
Augusten Stra 36
70178 Stuttgart, Germany
011-49-711-626-351

Dugina, Olga, 194
Augusten Stra 36
70178 Stuttgart, Germany
011-49-711-626-351

Duranceau, Suzanne, 348
4899 Sherbrooke W. #2
Westmount, Quebec H3Z 1H2
Canada
1-(514) 484-6229

Ehlert, Lois, 160, 200
839 N. Marshall St. #57
Milwaukee, WI 53202-3939
(414) 276-8336

Eidrigevicius, Stasys, 252
Bednarska 27, 00321
Warsaw, Poland
Rep. (212) 289-5514

Ellis, Steve, 260
93 Second Ave. #2
New York, NY 10003
(212) 979-0179

Elwell, Tristan, 41, 165
188 E. 80th St. #3B
New York, NY 10021
(212) 734-3353

Endewelt, Jack, 3
50 Riverside Dr.
New York, NY 10024
(212) 877-0575

English, John, 351, 398
5844 Fontana Dr.
Fairway, KS 66205
(913) 831-4830

English, Mark, 177, 265, 438
512 Lakeside Ct.
Liberty, MO 64068
(816) 781-0056

Fancher, Lou, 313
440 Sheridan Ave. S.
Minneapolis, MN 55405
(612) 377-8728

Farley, Malcolm, 343
7625 Quartz St.
Golden, CO 80403
(303) 420-9135

Fasolino, Teresa, 84, 152
233 E. 21st St. #6
New York, NY 10010
(212) 533-5543
Rep: (212) 260-6700

Ferry, John, 47, 48, 344
4957 Booth
Westwood, KS 66205
(913) 362-1581

Fiedler, Joseph Daniel, 57, 253, 256
921 Beech Ave. #3
Pittsburgh, PA 15233
(412) 243-0720
Rep: (212) 397-7330

Flesher, Vivienne, 163, 263, 327, 346, 349
(415) 921-2440
(212) 575-0064

Forbes, Bart, 46, 347, 350
5323 Montrose Dr.
Dallas, TX 75209
(214) 357-8077

Fredrickson, Mark, 53
5093 East Patricia St.
Tucson, AZ 85712
(602) 323-3179

French, Lisa, 259
355 Molino Ave.
Long Beach, CA 90814
(310) 434-5277

Fuchs, Bernie, 437
3 Tanglewood Ln.
Westport, CT 06880
(203) 227-4644

Gall, Chris, 94, 164
4421 N. Camino Del Santo
Tucson, AZ 85718
(602) 299-4454

Garns, Allen, 50
209 W. First Ave.
Mesa, AZ 85210
(602) 835-5769

Garro, Mark, 285
13 Richard St.
White Plains, NY 10603
(914) 946-7499

Gauthier, Corbert, 266
4073 Utica Ave., S.
St. Louis Park, MN 55416
(612) 926-1096

Giancola, Donato, 161
67 Dean St. #3
Brooklyn, NY 11201
(718) 797-2438

Giusti, Robert, 216, 217, 357, 406
340 Long Mountain Rd.
New Milford, CT 06776
(203) 354-6539
Rep: (212) 260-6700

Glaser, Milton, 258
207 E. 32nd St.
New York, NY 10016
(212) 889-3161

Glover, Ann, 359
1308 Factory Place #4B/Box 25
Los Angeles, CA 90013-2256
(213) 623-6203
Rep: (703) 343-7411

Goines, David Lance, 254
1703 M.L.K.Way
Berkeley, CA 94709
(510) 549-1405

Goldstrom, Robert, 70, 135
471 Fifth St.
Brooklyn, NY 11215
(718) 237-2784

Goodell, Brad, 262
605 Arizona SE
Albuquerque, NM 87108
(505) 255-7889

Goodrich Carter, 212
100 Angell St.
Providence, RI 02906
(800) 992-4552

Gorey, Edward, 73
8 Strawberry Ln.
Yarmouthport, MA 02675
(508) 362-3909

GrandPré, Mary, 317, 355
433 Holly Ave.
St. Paul, MN 55102
(612) 224-8576

Graves, Keith, 261, 281
1403 Pinewood Cove
Leander, TX 78641
(512) 259-8586

Griesbach, Cheryl, 424
41 Twinlight Terr.
Highlands, NJ 07732
(908) 291-5945

Grimes, Melissa, 278
901 Cumberland Rd.
Austin, TX 78704
(512) 445-2398

Grove, David, 62
382 Union St.
San Francisco, CA 94133
(415) 433-2100

Gurney, James, 339, 340, 352
PO Box 693
Rhinebeck, NY 12572
(914) 876-7746

Hatcher, Lois, 276
6035 Wyandotte
Kansas City, MO 64113
(816) 361-6230

Helton, Linda, 428
7000 Meadow Lake
Dallas, TX 75214
(214) 319-7877

ARTIST INDEX

Henderson, Hayes, 284
815 Burke St.
Winston-Salem, NC 27101
(910) 748-1364

Hendler, Sandra, 125
1823 Spruce St.
Philadelphia, PA 19103
(215) 735-7380

Hersey, John, 208
330 Sir Frances Drake Blvd.
San Anselmo, CA 94960
(415) 454-0771

Hillenbrand, Will, 353
808 Lexington
Terrace Park, OH 45174
(513) 831-5830

Hirschfeld, Al, 421, 422
122 E. 95th St.
New York, NY 10028
(212) 534-6172

Hoffman, Eugene, 236
1811 12th St.
Greeley, CO 80631
(303) 351-7991

Holland, Brad, 58, 77, 81,
  286, 287
96 Greene St.
New York, NY 10012
(212) 226-3675

Holly, Jason, 271
852 Monterey Rd.
South Pasadena, CA 91030
(818) 403-0152

Howard, John H., 56, 273,
  275, 358
270 Park Ave. South #8E
New York, NY 10010
(212) 260-6700

Hussey, Tim, 66
22 So. Battery
Charlston, SC 29401
(803) 722-7435

Isip, Jordin, 65
44 Fourth Pl. #2
Brooklyn, NY 11231
(718) 624-6538

Ito, Yoriko, 229
1706 Dolores St.
San Francisco, CA 94100
(415) 641-8041
Rep: (415) 641-8041

James, Bill, 13, 61
15840 S.W. 79th Ct.
Miami, FL 33157
(305) 238-5709

Jarecka, Danuta, 74
114 E. 7 St. #15
New York, NY 10009
(212) 353-3298

Jessell, Tim, 126
1906 Wedgewood Ct.
Stillwater, OK 74075
(405) 377-3619

Jetter, Frances, 136
2211 Broadway
New York, NY 10024
(212) 580-3720

Jinks, John, 274
27 W. 20th St. #1106
New York, NY 10011
(212) 675-2961

Johnson, David, 64, 371
New Canaan, CT
(203) 966-3269
Rep: Richard Solomon
(212) 683-1362

Johnson, Joel Peter, 91, 175
PO Box 803 Ellicott Station
Buffalo, NY 14205
(716) 881-1757

Johnson, Stephen T., 83
81 Remsen St. #1
Brooklyn, NY 11201
(718) 237-2352

Johnson, Steve, 313
440 Sheridan Ave. South
Minneapolis, MN 55405
(612) 377-8728

Joyce, William, 145, 146, 228
3302 Centenary Blvd.
Shreveport, LA 71104
(318) 869-0180

Kahl, David, 232
551 Observer Hwy. #12G
Hoboken, NJ 07030
(201) 963-7975

Kelley, Gary, 71, 80, 167, 269,
  328, 360
Cedar Falls, IA
(319) 277-2330
Rep: Richard Solomon
(212) 683-1362

Kimak, James, 69
20 Broadway
Piermont, NY 10968
(914) 359-1158

Koelsch, Michael, 181
9655 Turtledove
Fountain Valley, CA 92709
(714) 962-4645

Kunz, Anita, 67, 364
230 Ontario St.
Toronto, Ontario M5A 2V5
Canada
1-(416) 364-3846

Kurtz, Mara, 75
322 Central Park West
New York, NY 10025
(212) 666-1453

Kurtz, Sasha, 75
322 Central Park West
New York, NY 10025
(212) 666-1453

La Fleur, Dave, 367
9121 E. 79th St.
Derby, KS 67037
(316) 788-0253

Lee, Paul, 362
5818 1/2 N. Figueroa
Los Angeles, CA 90042
(213) 257-5618
Rep: (408) 372-4672

Leech, Richard, 419, 420
16 El Rincon Ave.
Orinda, CA 94563
(510) 254-5748

Lewis, H. B., 230
16 Canonchet Rd.
Hope Valley, RI 02832
(800) 522-1377

Liepke, Skip, 7, 60, 76,
  78, 173, 174
30 W. 72nd St. #2B
New York, NY 10023
Rep. (212) 683-1362

Lindlof, Ed, 168
603 Carolyn Ave.
Austin, TX 78705
(512) 472-0195

Livingston, Francis, 90
218 Willow Way Rd.
Hailey, ID 83333
(208) 788-1532

Locke, Gary, 365
1005 Woodruff Bldg.
Springfield, MO 65806
(417) 866-2885

LoFaro, Jerry, 201, 270
57 Laight St. 4th Fl.
New York, NY 10013
(212) 941-7936

Low, William, 106
c/o Vicki Morgan Assoc.
194 Third Ave.
New York, NY 10003
(212) 475-0440

Lukova, Luba, 79
1315 Second Ave. #5C
New York, NY 10021
(212) 861-1436

Maggard III, John P., 372,
  388, 435
102 Marian Ln.
Terrace Park, OH 45174
(513) 248-1550

Magsig, Stephen, 408
240 W. Maplehurst
Ferndale, MI 48220
(810) 398-4089

Mahurin, Matt, 68, 82
666 Greenwich St. #PH16
New York, NY 10014
(212) 691-5115

Manchess, Gregory, 4, 277, 370,
  376, 377
Beaverton, OR
(503) 590-5447
Rep: Richard Solomon
(212) 683-1362

Marshall, Dan, 320
41 Madison Ave.
New York, NY 10010
(212) 683-0001

Martinez, Sergio, 184, 378
c/o Spiers
43 E. 19th St.
New York, NY 10003
(212) 254-4996

Martucci, Stanley, 424
41 Twinlight Terr.
Highlands, NJ 07732
(908) 291-5945

Mathews, Adam, 297
142 Bickley Rd.
Glenside, PA 19038
(215) 884-9247

Matteson, Marvin, 188,
  223, 322
37 Cary Rd.
Great Neck, NY 11021
(516) 487-1323

Mayer, Bill, 121, 299, 311, 429
240 Forkner Dr.
Decatur, GA 30030
(404) 378-0686

McElmurry, Jill, 226
5829 Sacramento Ave.
Dunsmuir, CA 96025
(916) 235-0532

McGinnis, Robert, 225
13 Arcadia Rd.
Greenwich, CT 06870
(203) 637-1259

ARTIST INDEX

McKean, Dave, 219
Ebony Oast, Stone-Cum-Ebony,
Tenterden, Kent, TN30CHY,
London, England
011-44-79-727-0032

McKowen, Scott, 237
428 Downie St., Stratford,
Ontario, N5A 1X7, Canada
Rep. (212) 289-5514

McLean, Wilson, 85, 87, 89, 189, 361
27 Montauk Highway
Art Village, Southampton,
NY 11968
(516) 283-4276

McMahon, Mark, 430, 431
321 S. Ridge Rd.
Lake Forest, IL 60045
(708) 295-2604

McMullan, James, 272, 280, 314
207 E. 32nd St.
New York, NY 10016
(212) 689-5527

Meikle, David W., 379, 380
1704 Wasatch Dr.
Salt Lake City, UT 84108
(801) 582-5324

Merrill, Christine Herman, 210
505 Walker Ave.
Baltimore, MD 21212
(410) 433-3126

Nelson, Bill, 290, 426
Richmond, VA
(804) 783-2602
Rep: Richard Solomon
(212) 683-1362

Neubecker, Robert, 382
505 E. 3rd Ave.
Salt Lake City, UT 84103
(801) 531-6999

Nickle, John, 179
298 7th Ave. #1
Brooklyn, NY 11215
(718) 788-7310

Novak, Tony, 291
5010 Idaho Ave.
Nashville, TN 37209
(615) 385-4368
Rep: (612) 825-7564

O'Brien, Tim, 187, 231, 294
480 13th St.
Brooklyn, NY 11215
(718) 832-1287

Odom, Mel, 221
252 W. 76th St.
New York, NY 10023
(212) 724-9320

Olbinski, Rafal, 5, 296, 375, 383
142 E. 35th St.
New York, NY 10016
(212) 532-4328

Ortega, José, 86, 387
131 Charlie Parker Pl. Ave. B
#1C, New York, NY 10028
(212) 228-2606

Otnes, Fred, 392, 412, 416
26 Chalburn Rd.
West Redding, CT 06896
(203) 938-2829

Palencar, John Jude, 227
249 Elm St.
Oberlin, OH 44074
(216) 774-7312

Paraskevas, Michael, 93, 95, 319, 390, 393
157 Tuckahoe Ln.
Southampton, NY 11968
(516) 287-1665

Park, W. B., 27
110 Park Ave. South
Winter Park, FL 32789
(407) 644-1553

Parker, Robert Andrew, 98, 99, 127
22 River Rd.
West Cornwall, CT 06796
(203) 672-0152

Patrick, John, 391
c/o Scott Hull Asoc.
68 E. Franklin St.
Dayton, OH 45459
(513) 433-8383

Patti, Joyce, 185
1203 1/2 Seal Way
Seal Beach, CA 90740
Rep. (212) 475-0440

Paul, Jim, 368
6822 Roe
Prairie Village, KS 66208
(816) 545-2460

Payne, C. F., 101, 102, 103, 292, 389
Cincinnati, OH
(513) 821-8009
Rep: Richard Solomon
(212) 683-1362

Pedersen, Judy, 215
15 McEwen St.
Warwick, NY 10990
(914) 987-1090

Pelavin, Daniel, 171
80 Varick St. #3B
New York, NY 10013
(212) 941-7418

Pericoli, Tullio, 114
Via Pestalozza 4
Milano 20131, Italy
011-39-2706-38776

Pinkney, Jerry, 182, 186
41 Furnace Dock Rd.
Croton on Hudson, NY 10520
(914) 271-5238

Piven, Hanoch, 2, 97
310 W. 22nd St. #4A
New York, NY 10011
(212) 691-5133

Plank, Michael, 410
5833 Monrovia,
Shawnee, KS 66216
(913) 631-7021

Polson, Steven, 369
225 E. 79th St.
New York, NY 10021
(212) 734-3917

Pratt, George, 298
320 7th Ave.
Brooklyn, NY 11215
(718) 768-6008

Risko, Robert, 55
155 W. 15th St. #4B
New York, NY 10011
(212) 255-2865

Roberts, Leslie, 323
13601 Ventura Blvd. #247
Sherman Oaks, CA 91423
(818) 995-3907
Rep: (301) 394-5031

Rosado, Carlos, 204
8161 Woodhaven Blvd.
Glendale, NY 11385
(718) 441-9120

Rose, David, 411
1623 N. Curson Ave.
Los Angeles, CA 90046
(213) 876-0038

Roth, Arnold, 122
157 W. 57th St. #904
New York, NY 10019
(212) 333-7606

Royter, Randall, 289, 312
1537 S. Main St.
Salt Lake City, UT 84115
(801) 484-0419

Rudnak, Theo, 104, 105, 363, 394, 395
c/o Renard Represents, Inc.
501 Fifth Ave.
New York, NY 10017
Rep: (212) 490-2450

Rush, John, 279, 295, 316
123 Kedzie St.
Evanston, IL 60202
(708) 869-2078

Ryden, Mark, 133, 139, 300
541 Ramona Ave.
Sierra Madre, CA 91024
(818) 303-3133

Sadowski, Wiktor, 172, 288, 301, 302
c/o Marlena Agency
211 E. 89th St. #A1
New York, NY 10128
Rep. (212) 289-5514

Salina, Joseph, 21
2255 B. Queen St. E. #321
Toronto, Ontario, M4E 1G3
Canada
1-(416) 699-4859

Sanjulian, Manuel P., 214
Zona Terramar Stiges,
Barcelona, Spain
Rep: (212) 254-4996

Sano, Kazuhiko, 318
105 Stadium Ave.
Mill Valley, CA 94941
(415) 381-6377

Santore, Charles, 207
138 South 20th St.
Philadelphia, PA 19083
(215) 563-0430

Sealock, Rick, 110, 111
112 C. 17th Ave. N.W.
Calgary, Alberta, T2M0MG
Canada
1-(403) 276-5428

Shannon, David, 134, 170, 190, 233
1328 W. Morningside Dr.
Burbank, CA 91506
(818) 563-6763

Silverman, Burt, 113, 396
324 W. 71st St.
New York, NY 10023
(212) 799-3399

Singer, Phillip, 191
620 S. Cannon Ave.
Lansdale, PA 19446
(215) 393-7386
Rep: (516) 487-1323

Sis, Peter, 115
252 Lafayette St.
New York, NY 10012
(212) 226-0912

Slonim, David, 309
232 South St.
Chesterfield, IN 46017
(317) 378-6511

ARTIST INDEX

Smith, Elwood H., 118, 397
2 Locust Grove Rd.
Rhinebeck, NY 12572
(914) 876-2358

Sohn, Agatha, 116
250 W. 19th St. #4M
New York, NY 10011
(212) 741-6854

Spalenka, Greg, 117, 119, 235
21303 San Miguel St.
Woodland Hills, CA 91364
(818) 992-5828

Sparkman, Gene, 293
c/o Anita Grien
155 East 38th St. #15H
New York, NY 10016
Rep: (212) 697-6170

Spirin, Gennady, 140
Princeton, NJ
(609) 497-1720
Rep: Richard Solomon
(212) 683-1362

Spransy, Tim, 403
214 Wolf Dr.
Dousmon, WI 53118
(414) 965-3961

Springs, John, 107
51 Pelham St.
London, SW72NJ, England

Stabin, Victor, 308
84-21 Midland Pkwy.
Jamaica Estates, NY 11432
(212) 243-7688

Steinberg, James, 414
24 Summer St.
Amherst, MA 01002
(413) 549-1932

Stermer, Dugald, 112, 129, 213, 399, 401
600 The Embarcadero #204
San Francisco, CA 94107
(415) 777-0110
Rep: (415) 441-4384

Stevens, Doug, 108
6055 Cedar Wood Dr.
Columbia, MD 21044
(301) 596-5955

Sulkowski, Joseph H., 109
212 Paddock Ln.
Nashville, TN 37205
(615) 352-5493

Sullivan, Robert M., 404
PO Box 1079 / 1650 Fleetwood Rd.
Cutchogue, NY 11935
(516) 734-7589

Sumichrast, Jozef, 400
465 S. Beverly Pl.
Lake Forest, IL 60045
(708) 295-0255

Summers, Mark, 25, 141, 151, 211, 218, 304
Ontario, Canada
1-(905) 689-6219
Rep: Richard Solomon
(212) 683-1362

Swales, Scott, 54
1019 Main St.
Phoenix, NY 13135
(315) 695-4519

Sweeny, Glynis, 132
526 S. Connecticut Ave.
Royal Oak, MI 48067
(810) 548-4381

Sweetman, Dan, 137
100 E. Highland Ave.
Sierra Madre, CA 91024
(818) 355-5883

Taga, Yasutaka, 195
925 Hiyodorizima,
Toyama, 930, Japan
011-81-764-31-6735

Tamura, David, 192
412 N. Midland Ave.
Upper Nyack, NY 10960
(914) 358-4704

Thompson, Ellen, 199
67 de Leon Circle
Franklin Park, NJ 08823
(908) 422-0233

Thompson, John, 381, 402
206 Haddonfield Dr.
DeWitt, NY 13214
(315) 449-1241

Tillinghast, David, 124
1003 Diamond Ave. #200
S. Pasadena, CA 91030
(818) 403-0991

Toelke, Cathleen, 196, 198
PO Box 487
Rhinebeck, NY 12572
(914) 876-8776

Torres, Carlos, 407
1139 Prospect Ave. #1D
Brooklyn, NY 11218
(718) 768-3296

Tucker, Greg, 417
1915 Lakeview SW
Albuquerque, NM 87105
(505) 873-3727

Tylden-Wright, Jenny, 193
c/o Arena
11 Kings Ridge Rd.
Long Valley, NJ 07853
Rep: (908) 813-8718

Unruh, Jack N., 51, 130, 238, 384, 385, 386
2706 Fairmount
Dallas, TX 75201
(214) 871-0187

Vallejo, Dorian, 203
39 Forest St.
Montclair, NJ 07042
(201) 509-2990

Van Allsburg, Chris, 222

Venti, Anthony Bacon, 413
25 Clarendon St.
Rockland, ME 04841
(207) 596-7660

Ventura, Andrea, 138
c/o Gerald & Cullen Rapp
108 E. 35th St.
New York, NY 10016
Rep: (212) 889-3337

Ventura, Marco J., 310
Via Bergognone, 31
Milan 20144, Italy
011-39-2-894-09784

von Buhler, Cynthia, 423
16 Ashford St.
Boston, MA 02134
(617) 783-2421

Weinman, Brad, 202
310 E. Santa Anita Ave. #F
Burbank, CA 91502
(818) 843-2249

Weisbecker, Philippe, 415
136 Waverly Pl.
New York, NY 10014
(212) 627-7963

White, Eric, 205, 206, 268
1142 Castro St.
San Francisco, CA 94114
(415) 821-3839

Williams, Kent, 6, 120, 123
102 Sidney Green St.
Chapel Hill, NC 27516
(919) 968-1496

Wilson, Russ, 303
1420 Flagler Ave.
Jacksonville, FL 32207
(904) 398-0018

Wilson, Will, 307
5511 Knollview Court
Baltimore, MD 21228
(410) 455-0715

Witschonke, Alan, 267
68 Agassiz Ave.
Belmont, MA 02178
(617) 484-8023

Wood, Rob, 224
17 Pinewood St.
Annapolis, MD 21401
(410) 266-6550

Woolley, Janet, 169
c/o Arena
11 Kings Ridge Rd.
Long Valley, NJ 07853
Rep: (908) 813-8718

Yaccarino, Dan, 405
95 Horatio St. #204
New York, NY 10014
(212) 675-5335

Yang, Eric T., 306
213 La France Ave. #F
Alhambra, CA 91801
(818) 284-4727

Ziemienski, Dennis, 418
19176 Old Winery Rd.
Sonoma, CA 95476
(707) 935-0357

INTERNATIONAL ARTIST INDEX

Akiyama, Takashi, 441
3-14-35 Shimo-Ochiai
Shinjuku-ku, Tokyo 161
Japan
011-81-3-3565-4316

Anderson, Wayne, 440, 442
One Melbourne Close
Kibworth Beauchamp
Leicestershire LE80JP
England
011-44-6-251-8952

Benavides, Tono, 467
Pradillo 42, 28002 Madrid
Spain
011-34-1-5864855

Bosi, Marco, 446, 447
Via Teodosio 12
20131 Milano
Italy
011-39-2-70637558

Budgen, Dennis, 444, 445
64 Capri Ave., N.W. Calgary
Alberta T2L 0H1
Canada
1-403-282-0031

Campion, Paul, 448
Nude Chickens Studio
Exchange Buildings
Upper Hinton Rd.
Bournemouth, Dorset
BH1 2HH
England
011-44-202-317014

D'altan, Paolo, 450
c/o Superstudio 13
Via Forcella 13
20144 Milano
Italy
011-39-2-58102001

Dhers, Cosa, 451
13 Rue Arthur Legoust
31500 Toulouse
France
011-33-61-268694

Eriksson, Jerker, 443
Master Nilsgatan 1
211 26 Malmoe
Sweden
011-46-40-300450

Fujita, Shinsaku, 452
5-25-4 Yoyogi, Shibuya-ku
Tokyo
Japan
011-81-3-3460-4343

Furuta, Tadao, 453, 455
5-33-3-503 Kyodo
Setagaya-ku, Tokyo 156
Japan
011-81-3-3426-2819

Ichimura, Junichi, 454
1-A Yggdrasil, 2-80 Gaiku
Wakamatsu, Kanazawa-shi
Ishikawa
Japan

Izutsu, Hiroyuki, 464
1-15-3 Nishisugamo
Toshima-ku, Tokyo 103
Japan
011-81-3-3940-5845

Kawada, Hisao, 449
1-51-7-1001 Hounan
Suginami-ku, Tokyo
Japan
011-81-3-5300-0752

Kiefer, Alfons, 460
Furtweg 5, 85716
Unterschleissheim
Germany
0049-89-310-3538

Kiuchi, Tatsuro, 456, 457
3-26-20 Takanodai
Nerima-ku, Tokyo 177
Japan
011-81-3-5393-0083

Langeder, Helmut, 462
Catalpa Design Inc.
1260 Rue University
Suite 103, Montreal
Quebec H3B 3B9
Canada
1-514-866-7484

Lindell, Tomas, 468
Kornhamnstorng 59
111 27 Stockholm
Sweden
011-46-8-201200

Lohlein, Henning, 461
Bristol Craft & Design Center
6 Leonard Lane, Bristol
B51 1EA
England
011-44-117-9299-077

Lynch, P.J., 479
86 Upper Lesson St.
Dublin 4
Ireland
011-353-1-6680317

Martinez, Ricardo, 463
Pradillo 42, 28002
Madrid
Spain
011-341-5864855

Milot, Rene, 458, 459, 488
49 Thorncliffe Park Dr., Suite
1604, Toronto, Ontario M4H 1J6
Canada
1-416-425-7726

Miura, Hitoshi, 466
3-2-105-806 Sunadabashi
Higashi-ku, Nagoya 461
Japan
011-81-52-722-3506

Nakayama, Hisako, 477, 478, 480
1747-3 Ori-Inatsu-cho
Mizunami-shi, Gifu
Japan
011-81-572-68-0837

Nine, Carlos, 469, 470, 490
Argentina
c/o Herb Spiers, SI International
43 E. 19th St., New York
NY 10003
212-254-4996

Ohno, Takashi, 483
47-7 Sakae-cho, Kita-ku
Tokyo
Japan
011-81-3-3912-6093

Posthuma, Thomas, 471
Weesperbinnenweg 7E
1398 PC, Muiden
Holland
011-3-1294261844

Ruth, Trevor, 472
80 Scott St., Beaumaris
Melbourne, Victoria 3193
Australia
011-61-3-95893734

Salina, Joseph, 481, 482
2255 B Queen St., E.
Suite 321, Toronto
Ontario M4E 1G3
Canada
1-416-699-4859

Sasaki, Goro, 474, 475, 476
6-12-3 Narashinodai
Funabashi-shi, Chiba
Japan
011-81-474-66-2411

Seki, Shun-ichi, 489
480-12 Eda-cho, Aoba-ku
Yokohama-shi, Kanagawa
Japan
011-81-45-911-9127

Sibthorp, Fletcher, 487
England
c/o Jacqueline Dedell Inc.
58 W. 15th St.
New York, NY 10011
(212) 741-2539

Taga, Yasutaka, 484, 485, 486
925 Hiyodorizima
Toyama 930
Japan
011-81-764-31-6735

Taxali, Gary, 473
1589 Lovelady Cresent
Mississauga, Ontario
L4W 2Y9
Canada
1-905-625-1079

Tomita, Ben, 494
2-9-8 Izumi, Suginami-ku
Tokyo
Japan
011-81-3-3322-5887

Watanabe, Fumio, 493
3-8-7-804 Nishikasai
Edogawa-ku, Tokyo
Japan
011-81-3-3675-8526

Willms, Russ, 465, 491
53 Tovey Cr., Victoria
British Columbia V9B 1A4
Canada
1-604-744-1231

Woolley, Janet, 492
England
c/o Alan Lynch, Arena
11 Kings Ridge Rd.
Long Valley, NJ 07853
908-813-8718

ART DIRECTORS, CLIENTS, AGENCIES

A

A&E Networks, The History Channel, 320
Accordino, Michael, 219
Ackerman & McQueen, 365
Acting Company, The, 237
Actors Theater of Louisville, 252
AIGA/Minnesota, 363
Alaska Magazine, 8
Alexander, Gunta, 170, 233
Alfred A. Knopf, 144, 149, 150, 166
Ambassador Cards, 276
American Cyanamid, 257
American Jury by Trial Foundation, 154
American Medical News, 110
American Showcase, 424
American Way, 34, 329, 373
Anderson, Gail, 45
Andreozzi, Lynn, 163
Andrews, Vaughn, 181, 202, 232
Angel Records/EMI Classics, 322
Ariel Inc., 270
Arlow, Arnie, 239, 315
Art Directors Club of Cincinnati, 389
Art Students League of New York, 293
Atheneum/Macmillan Publishing Co., 198
Atlantic Monthly, The, 56, 65, 70, 71, 95, 97, 104, 138, 349
Avchen, Leslee, 401
AVIA, 238
Avon Books, 165, 201, 203

B

Bacilek, Tracy, 274
Bader Rutter & Assoc., Inc., 249
Bahm, Darwin, 381
Baker, Richard, 2, 42, 66, 107
Ballantine Books, 157
Balogh, Dennis, 16
Baltimore City Paper, 132
Bamford, David, 176
Bankers Trust, 286
Bantam Books, 205, 206, 255, 265
Bantam Doubleday Dell, 229
Barbieri, Jay, 322
Barker, Paul, 410
Barnard, Bryn, 332
Barnes & Noble, 141, 151, 211, 218
Bartels & Co., 429
Bartels, David, 300, 429
Bartels, Inc., 300
Barton, Harriett, 210
Bass, Wendy, 192, 198
Batteau, Wendy, 325, 427, 432, 433
Bauman, Leslie, 230
Beacon Magazine, 16, 305
Beckett Paper Co., 417
Bedell Cellars, 404
Bedell, Kip, 404
Behm, Kim, 247
Bender, Don, 207
Berg, Mathias, 194
Berkley Publishing Group, 176, 225, 227
Beyn, Bob, 324
Bhandari, Sunil, 364
Bide-A-Wee, 390
Bierhorst, Jane Byers, 215
Bierut, Michael, 147, 385
Bjornson, Becky, 266
Blake, Beverly, 49
Blassi, Jordi, 216, 217
Bon Marché, The, 284
Borman, Bill, 369
Borman Communications, 369
Boulton, Lynn, 143, 158
Boys' Life, 30, 46
Branson Theater L.P., 295
Braswell, Lynn, 229
Brooks, Scott, 270
Brower, Steven, 221
Brown, Bruce, 413
Bruce McGaw Graphics, 350
Brunell, Janice, 280
Budney, Dee Ann, 235
Bugle Boy Industries, 306
BUH Communicatie Adviesbureau, 358
Building Profit, 388
Burdett, Mark, 275
Business Information Group, The, 321
Bute, Eric, 289
Butler, Craig, 245, 317, 395

C

Cain, Tim, 130
Caleb, Mark, 175
Calver, Lewis, 59
Capaldi, Jef, 110
Capici, Amid, 101
Carillon Importers, 315
Carnegie Corp., 396
Carol Publishing Group, 221
Carver, Laurie, 318
Cedar Falls Chamber of Commerce, 247
Cellular One, 273
Center Stage, 301, 302
Champion International Corp., 353
Chiang, Albert, 51
Chicago Tribune Magazine, 118
Chief Executive, 74
Choice Printing, 236
Christensen, Mike, 62
Cincinnati Heart Assoc., 372
Citron Haligman Bedecarré, 235, 238
CKS Partners, 313
Clarity Coverdale Fury, 232
Cohen, Nancy, 75
Comiskey, Mike, 285
Comiskey, Roy, 6
Communication Arts/Rabbit Ears, 327, 346
Condon, Jim, 31
Connaster, Steve, 7
Connolly, Joseph P., 30, 46
Continuing Education/ University of Utah, 379, 380
Coonts, Bob, 236
Cornell, George, 180, 188
Counihan, Jerry, 214
Coverdale, Jac, 282
Covey Leadership Center, 62
Coyne, Patrick, 327, 346
Creative Editions, 155, 156, 178
Creative Living, 29
Cronin, Denise, 144, 149, 150, 166
Crossley, Greg, 290
Cuccurito, David, 78
Currie, Cynthia, 126
Curry, Christine, 12, 15, 26, 83, 98, 99, 114, 127, 128

D

Dallas Society of Visual Communications, 386
Daugherty, Bob, 249
Davy, Greg, 411
Dayton's Dept. Store, 328
DCE Design, 380
Dean, Bruce, 248
deCesare, John, 392
Degenhardt, Alice, 29
Delessert, Etienne, 326
Dell Publishing, 163, 214
Dial Books, 182, 186
Dial Books for Young Readers, 140
Diiola, Mike, 78
Dimos, Dennis Michael, 394
Discovery Communications Inc., 307
DNP America, Inc., 439
Doe, Kelly, 93, 103
Doherty, Noreen, 414
Dorritie Lyons & Nickel, Inc., 409
Dow Chemical, 249
Drace, Matthew, 112
Drescher, Henrik, 148
Drummond, Stacy, 275
Dubov, Gail, 201
Duckworth, Nancy, 54, 111
Du Pont Pharmaceuticals, 318
Duranceau, Suzanne, 348

E

Early, Mare, 118
Earthquake NYC, 285
Eddie Bauer, 269
Egner, Tom, 165, 203
Ekizian, David, 284
Ekizian Design, 284
Eleanor Ettinger Gallery, The, 173, 174, 279
Elfin Light Press, 184, 378
Elliot, Paul, 327, 346, 371
Engle, Mary Bess, 185
English, John, 398
Erwin Music, 250
Esquire, 101

F

Farago Advertising Inc., 290
Farley, Malcolm, 343
Farmer, Michael, 160, 196, 424
Federal Express, 105
Federal Reserve Bank of Dallas, 428
Federation des Cooperatives Migros, 244
Field & Stream, 109, 122, 129
Fili, Louise, 325, 427, 432, 433
Fitzgerald, Julie, 393
F.J.C. and N., 289, 312
Flinchum, Dwayne J., 4, 44, 58, 77, 89, 120
Flou, 310
Flynn-Hanrahan, Debra, 349
Flynn, Patrick, 136
Focus on the Family, 309
Foote Cone & Belding, 277
Forbes, 84
Ford Motor Co., 304
Forecast, 91
Fortuno, Anthony, 411
Four Seasons Hotel, 360
Four Seasons Hotels & Resorts Magazine, 36
Frankel, Margot, 23
Franklin & Nourzad, 278
Friedman, Ellen, 162, 199, 220
Friedman, Joni, 225
Friends of the Sebastiani Theater, 418
Froelich, Janet, 52, 135

G

Gail Imstepf, 124
Galerie Vallotton, 326
Galiloto, Rose, 91
Garguilo, Salvatore, 296
Garlan, Judy, 56, 65, 70, 71, 95, 97, 104, 138
GDS, 300
Geering, Martha, 40

ART DIRECTORS, CLIENTS, AGENCIES

General Motors/Saturn, 397
Gerani, Gary, 337
Gilmore-Barnes, Robin, 56, 138
Glickman, Corey, 253, 256
Gluth Weaver, 341, 342
Goines, David Lance, 254
Golden, David, 318
Gonzales, Gail, 406
Grafica Magazine, 412, 416
Grahl, Spencer, 43
Grand Lodge of New York, 369
Grand Marnier, 239
GrandPré, Mary, 355
Graphic Artists Guild, 208
Graphic-Sha, Inc., 195
Greenberg, Gary, 292
Greenwich Workshop, The, 338, 339, 340, 352
Greer, Mark, 333
Greer, Scott, 379, 380
Grosspietsch, Tom, 273
Grove/Atlantic, 159
GTI, 358

H
Hadassah, 400
Hallmark Cards, 368, 410
Hamilton, Carver & Lee, 318
Hansen, Christina, 8
Hansen, Jeri, 142, 197, 234
Harcourt Brace & Co., 148, 160, 181, 196, 202, 232
HarperCollins, 145, 146, 164, 200, 210, 213, 222, 228
Harris & Bhandari, 364
Harris, Neil, 268
Hartman, Bruce, 177, 438
Hayes, Emily, 147
HealthQuest, 116
Hearst Center for the Arts, 167
Helfand, Jessica, 86
Heller, Steve, 25
Helton, Linda, 428
Hendel, Rich, 168
Hernandez, Lynn, 415
Herrman, Carl, 345
Hess, Charles, 115
Hess, Mark, 357
Hillenbrand, William, 353, 388
Hill Holiday, 414
Himmel, Sheila, 134
Hinrichs, Kit, 399
Hochstein, Arthur, 21, 53, 72, 88, 92, 102
Hohl, Susan R., 405
Hollander, Sara, 90
Honda, Kimio, 439
Houghton Mifflin, 175
How, Belle, 272
Huber, Paul, 397
Hug, Charlotte, 244
Hull, Scott, 435
Hurlbut, Angie, 321
Hyperion Books, 193
Hyperion Books for Children, 162, 199, 220

I
Image Bank/Film, 290
Indianapolis Repertory Theatre, 248
Iowa Alliance For Arts Education, 254
Islands, 51

J
Jacksonville Convention and Visitors Bureau, 303
John Hancock, 414
Johnson Controls, Inc., 316
Johnson County Cultural Center, 177, 438
Johnson, Scott, 248
Jones, Laura, 374
Jones, Tim, 309

K
Kansas City Magazine, 48
Kascht, John, 108
K. D'Addario, 298
Kehoe, Kevin, 283
Kelley, Gary, 76, 167
Kelly, John, 141, 151, 211, 218
Kesel, Mick, 299, 311
Kettner, Christine, 145, 146, 228
Killian's Red Beer, 277
Kimak, James, 69
Kiplinger's Personal Finance Magazine, 126, 130
Klaetke, Fritz, 423
Klem, Tina, 36
Klugerman, Barry, 184, 378
Kocaurek, Lisa, 79
Koester, Ken, 386
Kohn, Norm, 242
Korpics, John, 38
Krenitsky, Nicholas, 164
Krules, Jean, 215
Krygier, Dorothy, 331
Kuisel, Mick, 259
Kushnirsky, Julia, 19, 94, 169
Kuypers, Christian, 14

L
Lambson, Don, 50
Lawson, Jennifer, 354
Lears, 57
Lebenson, Richard, 223
Lehmann-Haupt, Carl, 75
Lentini, Tony, 341, 342
Levi, Lauren, 121
Lewis, Irene, 301, 302
Liepke, Skip, 173, 174
Lifetouch Publishing, 266
Lin, Clifton, 294
Lincoln Center Theater, 280, 314
Lindgren & Smith, 319
Lintas Campbell Ewald, 299, 311
Littleton 2, 374
Live Oak Theater, 278
L.L. Bean, 354
London/Polygram, 268
Lopez, Andrew, 306
Los Angeles County Transportation Authority, 411
Los Angeles Times, The, 17
Los Angeles Times Calendar, 137
Los Angeles Times Magazine, 54, 111
Louisville Graphic Design Assoc., The, 330
Luger, Diane, 212

M
Macmillan Inc., 192, 215, 325, 427, 432, 433
Macuga, Sam, 257
Maine Coast Artists, 413
Makon, Joy, 64
Mansfield, Bob, 84
Marino, Guy, 286
Mark Taper Forum, 288
Marshall, Alisann, 34, 329, 373
Marshall, Dan, 320
Marshall Jaccoma Mitchell, 320
Marshall, Rita, 155, 156, 178, 425
Maser Galleries, 437
Maser, Ron, 437
Matsunaga, Shin, 263
Matsuzaki, Shoji, 361, 439
Mattel, 139
Mattelson, Marvin, 260
Maurer, Mary, 271
MBI, 331
McFadden, Lori, 269
McGinty, Tricia, 33, 119
McKowen, Scott, 237
McPhail, Jerry, 384
Melis, Franka, 358
Memorial Healthcare System, 333
Mercury House, 226
Merkley, Newman & Harty, 286
Metropolis, 75
Metz, Frank, 153
Meyer, Jackie Merri, 152, 189
Mezzo, Cathryn, 5, 11, 67, 123, 375
Miller Kadanoff, 397
Milwaukee Magazine, 106, 117
Mimnaugh, George, 132
Miranda, Oswaldo, 412, 416
Mitchell Energy Development Corp., 341, 342
Mitchell, Steve, 309
Mohawk Paper, 147, 385
Monterey Bay Aquarium, 399, 406
Moody Magazine, 43
Mortgage Banking, 90
Mother Jones Magazine, 10
Mouly, Francoise, 37
Ms., 79
Multhauf, Mary, 117
Murello, Judith, 227

N
Nature Co., 261, 281
Nead, Richard, 291
Nelson, Bill, 426
Nelson, Sharon, 106
New American Library, 188
Newborn Group, The, 357
New Jersey State Council on the Arts, 332, 402
New Woman, 33, 119
New York City Opera, 296, 383
New Yorker, The, 12, 15, 26, 37, 83, 98, 99, 114, 127, 128
New York Times, The, 135
New York Times Magazine, The, 25, 52
Norm Kohn Studio, 242
North American Review, The, 76
Northwestern National Life, 282
Norwegian Cruise Line, 313
Nourzad, M. P., 278
NRA, 365

O
OEM Magazine, 63
Ohye, Jan, 383
Olding, Denise, 330
O'Mara, Sharyn, 351
Omni, 4, 5, 11, 67, 123
Open Hand, 235
Orion Capital Corp., 436
Ost, Bill, 276
Outrigger Hotels Hawaii, 259, 299, 311
Owens, Don, 154
Oxford University Press, 171

P
Paine, Howard E., 419, 420, 421, 422
Paraskevas, Michael, 319, 390, 393
Parisi, Elizabeth B., 187, 231
Parker, Fred, 418
Parkinson, John, 304
Passehl, Chris, 436
Patrick, John, 391
Paul, Jim, 368
Pearlman, Robert, 400
Penguin USA, 161, 180, 224

ART DIRECTORS, CLIENTS, AGENCIES

Penthouse, 44, 58, 77, 78, 89, 120
Pepe, Paolo, 179
Perrier, 274
Pettit, Scott, 243
Pfeffer, Daniel, 57
Pfizer Inc., 409
Phelps, Lynn, 363
Philadelphia Inquirer, 86
Phipps, Alma, 74
Piplits, Erwin, 287
Playboy, 9, 47, 85
Plumeri, Jim, 255, 265
P.M.S., 403
Pocket Books, 179
Pope, Kerig, 9, 85
Porter, J., 32
Port of Seattle Communication, 415
Post, Doug, 236
Pracher, Rick, 159
Praiss, Laura A., 409
Premiere, 38
Private Clubs, 7
Prodigy, 69
Progressive, The, 136
P.S.J. Warsaw, 375
Pullum, Bob, 238
Pulse Magazine, 59
Putnam, 170, 233

Q
Q1 Communicators, 270

R
Rabbit Ears Productions, 371
Racs, Pam, 288
Rafferty, John, 298
Rainforest Alliance, 294
Ramji-Stein, Mira, 63
Random House Value Publishing, Inc., 207
Raphael Hotel Group, The, 351
Reece Galleries, 392
Reed, Dawn, 430, 431
Reed Interior Design, 430, 431
Reed, Tom, 430, 431
Reinhard, Matt, 277
Rhea & Kaiser Adverting, Inc., 243
Rhone-Poulenc Ag Co., 243
Richard Solomon Artists Representative, 370, 377, 426
Richer, Paul, 41
Ring, Melissa, 207
Robins, Kaplan, Miller & Ciresi, 291
Rocky Mountain Magazine, 80
Rogers, Lilla, 267
Rolling Stone, 20, 22, 45, 55, 60, 68, 96
Ross, Ben, 389
Ross, Ruth, 157

Rossin, Greenberg, Seronick, 292
RSVP, 223
Rumreich, Sandy, 105
Rush, John, 295
Russek Advertising Inc., 280, 314
Russek, Jim, 314
Russell, Avery, 396

S
Salz, Ina, 28, 73
Sanford, John Lyle, 307
Sarah Bain Gallery, 362
Savini, Jill, 313
Scholastic Inc., 64, 187, 190, 191, 231
Schwandner, Cliff, 372
Schwandner, Kris, 372
Scopin, Joe, 108
Scott Hull Assoc., 355, 374, 391, 435
Seacat, James, 252
Security Management Magazine, 6
Seraphein Beyn, 324
Serapions Theatre, 287
Sesame Street Magazine, 41
Sganzerla, Angelo, 310
Shantic, Diana, 17, 137
Shattuck, Laurie, 100
Shiseido, 263
Shlafer, Jonathan, 285
Siegfried, Elizabeth, 403
Sierra, 40
Simon & Schuster, 153, 185
Simpson Paper, 272
Sive Young & Rubicam, 294
Smith, Anissa, 116
Smith, Kenneth, 21, 53, 72, 88, 113
Smith, Sharon, 226
Society of Illustrators, 425
Solomon, Richard, 370, 377
Sommers, Joan, 172, 209
Sony Music, 271, 275
Soteropulos, Connie, 328
Southampton Hospital, 393
Spin, 82
Squires, Sheri, 330
St. Martin's Press, 183, 204, 219
Stabin, Victor, 308
Stack, Nina, 301, 302
Staebler, Tom, 9, 47
Stagmeister, S., 360
Stanton, Mindy Phelps, 109
Starace, Tom, 200, 222
Stout, D. J., 1, 18, 39, 81, 125
Stratus, 292
Stroman, Randy, 312
Stuart, Neil, 224
Stucky, Ron, 382

Studio'Mara, 351
Sturgis, Frank, 435
Sunrise Publications Inc., 348
Swanson, Kevin, 48

T
20/30 Club Equestrian Fundraiser, 262
29th St. Theater Co., 308
Taback, Simms, 208
Tackett, Harold, 241
Tan, John, 122, 129
Tavern and Top Deck, The, 398
TBWA Advertising, 239
Tehon, Atha, 140, 182, 186
Texas Monthly, 1, 18, 39, 81, 125
Texas Realtor, 121
Thomasson-Grant, 194
Thompson, Steve, 316
Tillinghast, David, 124
Time, 14, 21, 53, 72, 88, 92, 102, 113, 133
Tinkelman, Murray, 347
Todd, Jerry, 161
Tomato, 258
Tommasino, David, 191
Topps Co., Inc., The, 337
Tora, Shinichiro, 195
Torello, Nicholas D., 64
Town & Country, 23
Travel & Leisure, 112
Traverrohback Inc., 316
Tremain, Kerry, 10
Tumbleweed Press, 343
Turner, Clay, 365
Turner Publishing, Inc., 143, 158

U
University of Chicago Press, The, 172, 209
University of Hawaii Press, 168
USC Health & Medicine, 115
U.S. Facilities Corp., 394
Usher, David, 338, 339, 340, 352
US magazine, 2, 42, 66, 107
U.S. Postal Service, 419, 420, 421, 422

V
Valentine Radford, Inc., 276
Vaughn, Rick, 417
Vaughn/Wedeen Creative, 417
Viking Penguin, 142, 197, 234
Virtue Magazine, 100
Volpicelli, Joe, 285
Von Boetticher, Leigh, 262
Von Boetticher, Linda, 262

W
Waegle, Janet, 133

Wagner, Lisa, 2
Wallace, Andrew, 289
Wall Street Journal, The, 31
Walton, Michele, 390
Warhola, James, 184, 378
Warner Books, 19, 94, 152, 169, 189, 212
Warner Brothers, 285
Washington Post Magazine, The, 93, 103
Washington Times, The, 108
Waxdeck Birdcalling, Contest, 429
Weaver, Gluth, 341, 342
Weaver, John, 341, 342
Weaver, Victor, 193
Weisbach, Rob, 205, 206
Wertz, Nora, 171
West Magazine, 134
Westray, Kathy, 190
White, Eric, 205, 206, 268
Wierdon, Sue, 315
Williams & Rockwood, 283
Wilson, Fo, 116
Wilson, Jim, 403
Wilson, Russ, 303
Wil Tel, 241
Wireless Design & Development, 49
Witham Fine Art, 376
Witham, Sherri, 376
Women's Guild of United Cerebral Palsy, 384
Woodward, Fred, 20, 22, 45, 55, 60, 68, 96
Woof Productions, 401
WordPerfect, 382
WordPerfect Magazine, 50
Workbook, The, 245, 317, 395
WorldFest, 242
Worth Magazine, 28, 73
WQED 13, 253
WQED FM, 256
Wrigley, Lisa, 80

Y
Yankee Magazine, 32
Yee, Henry Sene, 183, 204
Yo, Craig, 139

Z
Z Group, The, 305
Zimmerman Crowe Design, 261, 281
Zimmerman, John, 305
Zimmerman, Neal, 261, 281
Zions Bank, 283
Zumbo, Matt, 403

INTERNATIONAL ART DIRECTORS, CLIENTS, AGENCIES

A
Achilles, 483
Akiyama, Takashi, 441
American Express International, 464
Anderson, Wayne, 442
Art Gallery Maya, 474, 476
Australian News Print Mills, 472

B
Bark, John, 468
Binzstock, J., 490
British Telecom, 487
Bungeishunju, 452

C
Caderot, Carmelo, 463, 467
Canadair, Fire Prevention, 458, 459
Carrot Gallery, The, 473
Carthusia Edizioni Srl, 446, 447
Codacons, 450
Cottage Life, 481
Crotty, Robert, 461

D
Daiwa-Syoken, 455
Dan, 448
Dekker, Jan, 451
Dorling Kindersley, 440

E
Eberth, David A., Dr., 444, 445
Edwards, Amelia, 479
El Mundo, 463, 467

F
Fairweather, Ronnie, 492
Fujinami, Madoka, 453
Fuzambo, 456, 457

H
Homecare Magazine, 465
Homemakers Magazine, 482

J
JAGDA, 466

K
Katharine Hamnett 469, 470
KDD Co., Ltd., 494
Kitanihon Broadcasting Co., Ltd., 485

M
Manley, Steve, 481
Marini, Lorenzo, 450
Matsuoka, Yusuke, 484, 486
Matsushita, Koichi, 494
Meiji Seimei Co., 493
Meingast, Susan, 482
Mitsui Insurance Co., Ltd., 475

Miura, Hitoshi, 466
Morgan, Marc, 469, 470
Murakami, Akira, 449

O
Okamoto, Issen, 464
Organon, 451

P
Penguin Group, 492
Pinpoint Gallery, 441
PNMD/Publitel, 462
Posthuma, Thomas, 471
Priddy, Roger, 440
Priority Man, 491

R
Revolver Music Ltd., 448
Royal Tyrrell Museum of Palaeontology, 444, 445
Roy, Pierre, 462

S
Saito, Masataka, 483
Sakuma, Yumiko, 456, 457
Sasaki, Goro, 474, 476
Schack, Peder, 443
Sevil Deu Nosse, 490
Smith, Gord, 488
Suruga Co., Ltd., 453

T
Tafelmusik, 488
Taga, Yasutaka, 485
Takarajimasha, Inc., 484, 486
Tanaka, Miwa, 493
Telia, 443
Tessier, Dominique, 458, 459
Thomas, Steve, 472
Tider, Moderna, 468
Toppan Printing Co., Ltd., 449
Tsukahara, Taiji, 455
Turner, Sue, 487
Typo's en Litho's, 471

V
Vnu Publishing, 461

W
Walker Books/Candlewick Press, 479
Willms, Russ, 491
Wizart, 442

Z
Zerbi, Patrizia, 446, 447

PROFESSIONAL STATEMENTS

DAVID BOWERS

CLIFF KNECHT
ARTIST REPRESENTATIVE

309 WALNUT ROAD PITTSBURGH, PA 15202 PHONE 412 • 761 • 5666   FAX 412 • 761 • 4072

Illustration

PHILIP ANDERSON
NANETTE BIERS
STUART BRIERS
LON BUSCH
JACK DAVIS
ROBERT DE MICHIELL
BILL DEVLIN
LEE DUGGAN
THE DYNAMIC DUO
JACKI GELB
RANDY GLASS
THOMAS HART
PETER HOEY
CELIA JOHNSON
STEVE KELLER
LASZLO KUBINYI
BERNARD MAISNER
HAL MAYFORTH
RICK MEYEROWITZ
BRUCE MORSER
ALEX MURAWSKI
MARLIES NAJAKA
SIGMUND PIFKO
CAMILLE PRZEWODEK
MARC ROSENTHAL
JAMES STEINBERG
DREW STRUZAN
ANDREA VENTURA
MICHAEL WITTE
BOB ZIERING

GERALD & CULLEN RAPP

We represent usually friendly somewhat DEMENTED wonderfully TALENTED illustrators. And have for over 50 years.

For a copy of our 50 page wire-bound talent portfolio, write us on your company letterhead. Sorry, outside the US or Canada send $10. int'l postal money order for shipping. Gerald & Cullen Rapp, 108 East 35 St. (#7) New York, NY 10016 Phone (212) 889-3337 Fax (212) 889-3341

PRIME
YOUR CANVAS

success means preparation . . .

To be prepared the student must:

- Know how to draw and design.

- Know how to generate great ideas.

- Know the various media and tools available to today's illustrator.

- Know how to produce and market professional level work.

At Savannah College of Art and Design, the illustration department's award - winning faculty not only prepares students to succeed, but to take their place among the finest in the field.

Call for a free catalog today!

Savannah College of Art and Design
Post Office Box 3146 · Savannah · Georgia 31402 - 3146
Telephone 1 800 869 SCAD
Fax 912 238 2456
EMail Admissions@SCAD.EDU

SCAD

B.F.A. M.F.A. M.A.
B.ARCH. M.ARCH.

Accredited by the Commission on Colleges
of the Southern Association of Colleges and Schools and the
National Architectural Accrediting Board

Gloria Elliott

Robert Casilla

Lyle Miller

Deborah DeSaix

Betsy Day

Kirchoff/Wohlberg

Artists Representatives

866 United Nations Plaza, New York, NY 10017
(212) 644-2020

Directory of Illustration

FOR MORE THAN 13 YEARS, THE DIRECTORY OF ILLUSTRATION HAS BEEN GENERATING BUSINESS FOR COMMERCIAL ARTISTS. WE TAKE THIS RESPONSIBILITY VERY SERIOUSLY.

ROBERT PASTRANA

ADVERTISING IN THE DIRECTORY OF ILLUSTRATION PLACES YOUR WORK AMONG THE BEST IN THE BUSINESS AND MONTHS AHEAD OF YOUR COMPETITION. TO RECEIVE A 16 PAGE BROCHURE ON THE DIRECTORY OF ILLUSTRATION #13, CALL 800-876-6425.

EARLY RESERVATIONS	MARCH 15, 1996
FINAL RESERVATIONS	APRIL 12, 1996
ARTWORK DUE	MAY 22, 1996
PUBLICATION DATE	NOVEMBER 1996

PUBLISHED BY SERBIN COMMUNICATIONS, INC.
511 OLIVE STREET
SANTA BARBARA, CA 93101 800-876-6425

Number Thirteen

WE BELIEVE THAT PERSONAL VISION NEED NOT BE THE EXCLUSIVE PROVINCE OF THE FINE ARTIST

MASTER OF FINE ARTS IN ILLUSTRATION AS VISUAL ESSAY

This unique two year Master of Fine Arts program in Illustration is offered to commercial and fine artists who want to broaden their abilities to create personal statements in pictures and words. It is designed to encourage a personal, artistic vision through the development of the visual essay. It is an opportunity to learn how visual stories are developed and combined with text specifically for publication and gallery walls. To visit the *Master of Fine Arts in Illustration As Visual Essay Program* and discuss the program in detail, please call (212) 645-0458 for an appointment.

FACULTY

MARSHALL ARISMAN
Chairman, Illustrator/Painter

GREGORY CRANE
Painter

PAUL DAVIS
Illustrator/Designer

LAURIE DOUGLAS
Computer Artist

CAROL FABRICATORE
Illustrator

MICHAEL FLANAGAN
Painter/Writer

STEVEN HELLER
Art Director

ELIZABETH HENLEY
Poet/Writer

CARL TITOLO
Painter

MARY JO VATH
Painter

THOMAS WOODRUFF
Illustrator/Painter

For further information call or write to the Office of Graduate Admissions

SCHOOL OF VISUAL ARTS
A COLLEGE OF THE ARTS

209 East 23rd Street, New York, NY 10010. (212) 592-2100 Fax (212) 725-3584.

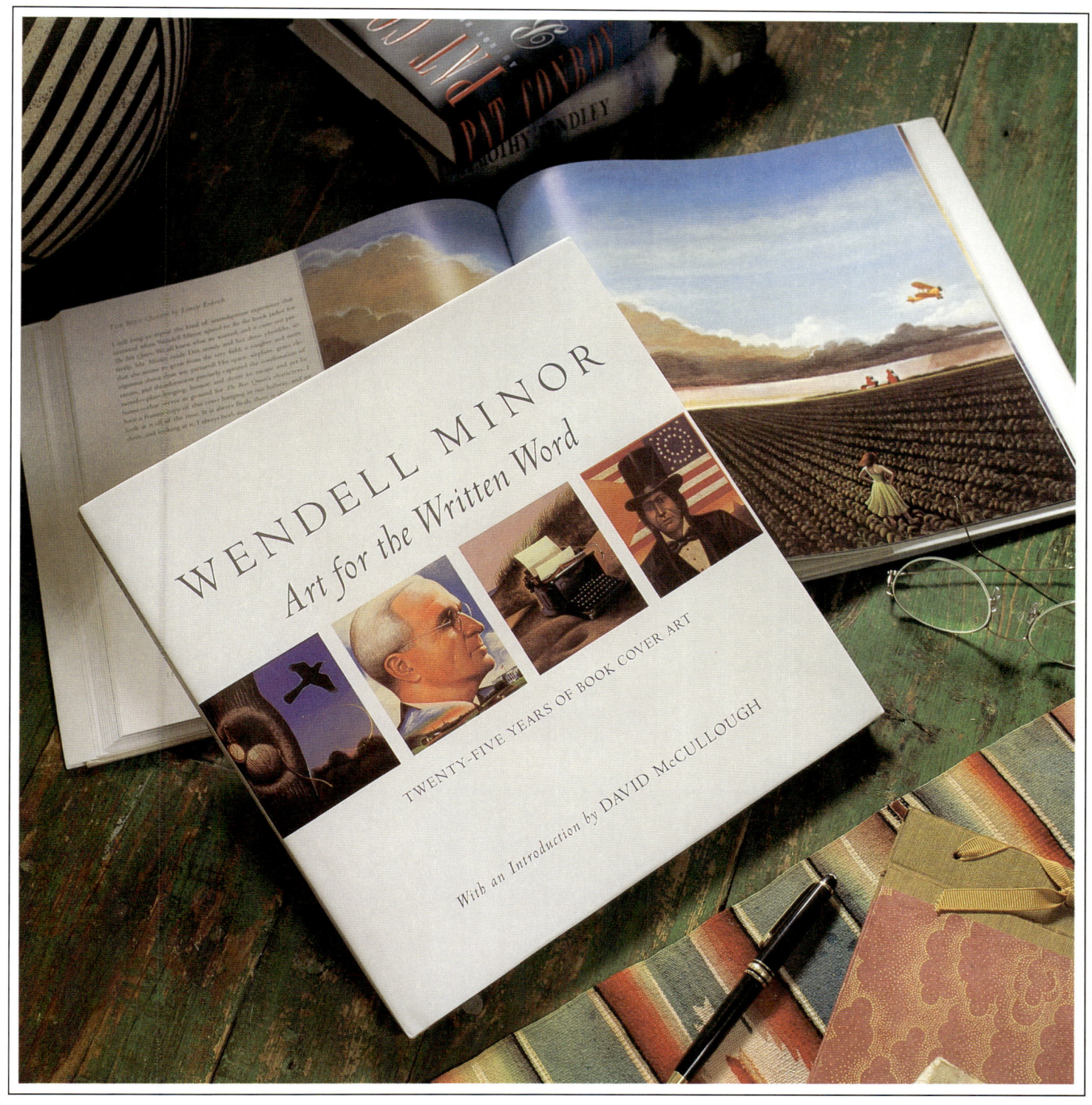

"In the world of publishing there is no one quite like Wendell Minor. Indeed, his value to the whole world of books, to publishers, editors, authors, booksellers, and to millions of readers who care about books, can hardly be overstated." — DAVID MCCULLOUGH

HARCOURT BRACE

WENDELL MINOR: ART FOR THE WRITTEN WORD
Available in paperback or hardcover collector's edition. At bookstores everywhere.

THE SUMMER OF 1995 WAS AN EXCITING TIME AT THE ILLUSTRATION ACADEMY. BELOW, INSTRUCTORS ARE GIVING DEMONSTRATIONS AND HELPING STUDENTS WITH THEIR WORK.

MARK ENGLISH

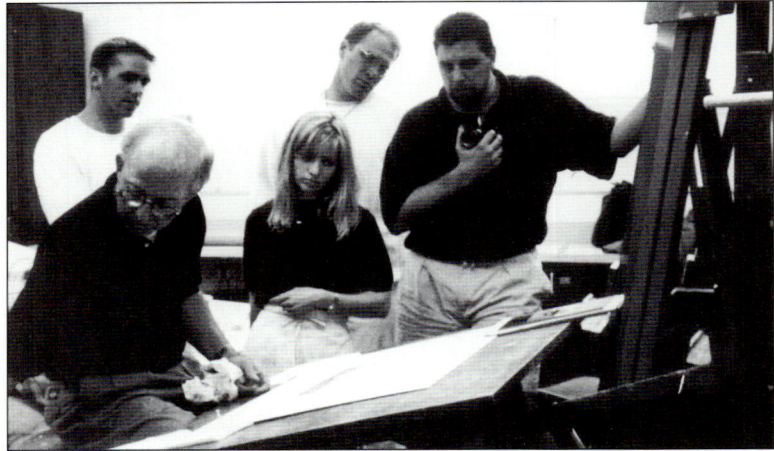

BART FORBES

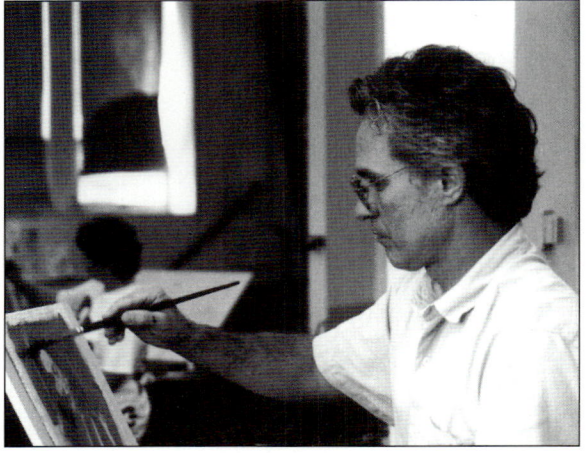

SKIP LIEPKE

CHRIS PAYNE

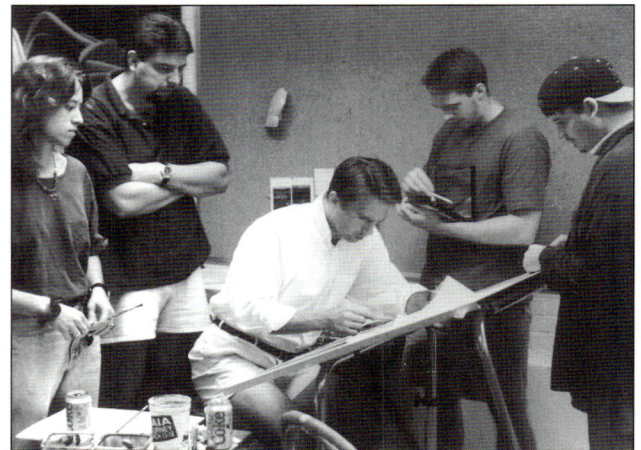

JOHN ENGLISH

JACK UNRUH

JOHN COLLIER

GARY KELLEY

**MARK ENGLISH
JOHN COLLIER
JOHN ENGLISH
BART FORBES
GARY KELLEY
ANITA KUNZ
SKIP LIEPKE
FRED OTNES
C.F. PAYNE
JACK UNRUH
BRENT WATKINSON**

THE ILLUSTRATION ACADEMY

THE ILLUSTRATION ACADEMY OFFERS ART STUDENTS AND PROFESSIONALS THE OPPORTUNITY TO STUDY WITH SOME OF THE MOST SUCCESSFUL AND EXCITING ILLUSTRATORS WORKING TODAY. SEE THE ART AND TALK TO THE ARTISTS WHO SET THE PACE IN THE FIELD. IMPROVE YOUR WORK, YOUR WORK HABITS, AND YOUR PORTFOLIOS.

THE ILLUSTRATION ACADEMY OFFERS A ONE-WEEK, AND TWO FOUR-WEEK INTENSIVE WORKSHOPS TO BE HELD IN THE SUMMER OF 1996 AT WILLIAM JEWELL COLLEGE IN LIBERTY, MISSOURI. ROOM AND BOARD ARE AVAILABLE; UP TO TWELVE HOURS OF COLLEGE CREDIT OFFERED THROUGH WILLIAM JEWELL COLLEGE.

MARK ENGLISH, CHRIS PAYNE AND STUDENTS ON CAMPUS.

ONE-WEEK SESSION
MAY 22 – 26

FIRST FOUR-WEEK SESSION
MAY 26 – JUNE 21

SECOND FOUR-WEEK SESSION
JUNE 23 – JULY 12

FOR MORE INFORMATION WRITE TO:
THE ILLUSTRATION ACADEMY
5844 FONTANA DRIVE
FAIRWAY, KS 66205

OR CALL:
913-789-8878

life:

A bed, bath, shelter, chocolate, work, coffee, a pad, a pen, direction, inspiration, self promotion, praise, fame, glory, dedication, money, closet organizer, a mate who can cook, a mate, sunshine, plants (for oxygen purposes only), care packages from Grandma, self promotion, an art director with taste, a pause button, ice cream, darts, self promotion, spicy tuna rolls, that trip to Bora Bora, someone to walk the damn dog, a massage, clean paint brushes, clean underwear, trust funds, a field trip to the petting zoo, uninhibited fun, a maid, a water gun, funkadelic, disco, line dancing, self promotion, discretionary income (yea right!), ego, super ego, id, 'sometimes Anna a cigar is just a cigar', a really good peach, a security blanket, a rep, speed dial, call forwarding, being right, oils that dry, a filling, self promotion, Paradise, 2 remote controls, jacks and super balls, basketball hoop behind bathroom door, a bathroom door, communication, a winning lottery ticket, chunky peanut butter, award winning illustration, time, thyme, a good license photo, toilet paper, a life, a great foot rub, self promotion, a muscle, computer, therapy, good vibes from Madame Zelda, a law degree, latte, a nice fishing hole, a rainbow, a pat on the back, breathmints, B movies, 60's tv, a scratch on the back, creative freedom, sex, deadline extensions, an executive assistant, brainfood, success, self promotion, self promotion, self promotion!

illustration: Brad Weinman

American Showcase.

915 BROADWAY 14TH FL NEW YORK NY 10010   212 673 6600   800 894 7469

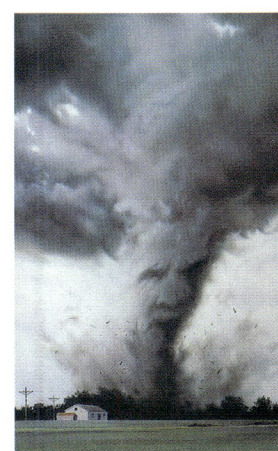

Wood Ronsaville Harlin, Inc.

Illustration to enhance your ideas. [410] 266-6550 Fax [410] 266-7309 We're the illustration studio with all of the artists on staff.

BALDING DISCO STUD ATTACKS PUNCTUATION MARKS WITH AN AX TO IMPRESS HOMELESS RUNWAY MODELS WITH BIG BARE BUTTOCKS.

- pages 84, 285, 446, 967.

1996 Workbook Illustration

what do you see?

EAST: (212) 674-1919 (800) 322-3470 • MIDWEST: (312) 944-7925 (800) 752-0285 • SOUTH: (505) 466-9634 (800) 346-5266 • WEST: (213) 856-0008 (800) 547-2688

JOHN THOMPSON
315 449 1241

THE ATLANTIC MONTHLY - Mary Workman A.D.

11 1/2 " x 30 " . Acrylic on masonite

DAM!

There are over 100,000 dams in this country. America is fast becoming one of the most dammed countries in the world second only to China.

ROBERT CRAWFORD
123 MINORTOWN RD. WOODBURY, CT 06798 (203)266-0059

CLEAN, WHITE
T-SHIRTS ADD STYLE
IN THE WORK PLACE,
OFFICE, HOME
OR STUDIO.
ORDER YOURS NOW.

$14.95

AVAILABLE IN
THE CONTINENTAL
USA ONLY.
NEW YORK STATE
RESIDENTS, PLEASE
ADD APPROPRIATE
SALES TAX.

Nice shirt Al. Want a raise?

OK, thanks Boss.

WHEN PLACING
YOUR ORDER
INDICATE SIZE
(L & XL ONLY),
QUANTITY, AND
ILLUSTRATOR #.
ADD $3.95 FOR
SHIPPING AND
HANDLING
PER ORDER,
ANY QUANITIY.

SEND PAYMENT
IN THE FORM OF
CASH (ALWAYS
NICE), CHECK OR
MONEY ORDER.
PAYABLE TO
G&C RAPP, INC.

Improve your appearance.
Improve your life.

S. BRIERS ❶	M. WITTE ❷	R. DE MICHIELL ❸	J. DAVIS ❹
M. ROSENTHAL ❺	DYNAMIC DUO ❻	H. MAYFORTH ❼	A. MURAWSKI ❽
B. MAISNER ❾	J. STEINBERG ❿	R. MEYEROWITZ ⓫	DREW ⓬

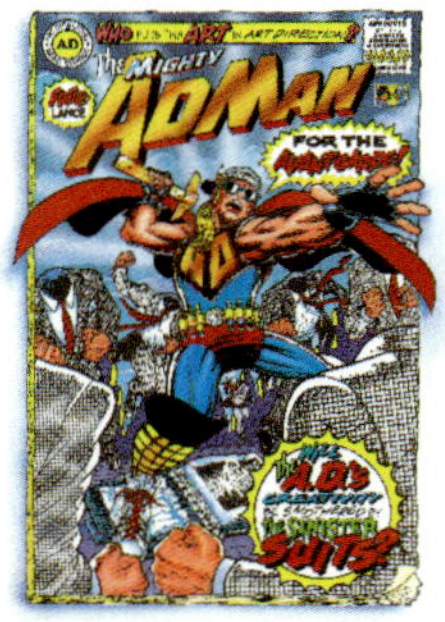

Gerald & Cullen Rapp, Inc. 108 East 35 St. (#7) New York, NY 10016

SOCIETY ACTIVITIES

The Society of Illustrators National Lecture Series

Through the generous support of Mobil Foundation, Inc., the Society has been able to bring nationally recognized illustrators to New York for "An Evening With...".

These informative, yet informal presentations in the casual, yet historical setting of the Society's Members Dining Room, have been videotaped and made available to college-level art programs nationwide.

What began in the 1930's as panel discussions to local artists by such luminaries as Norman Rockwell, James Montgomery Flagg and Charles Dana Gibson, are now a national forum for today's top illustrators.

The Society expresses its deep appreciation to the MOBIL FOUNDATION for its six consecutive years of support. Through them we have gone national.

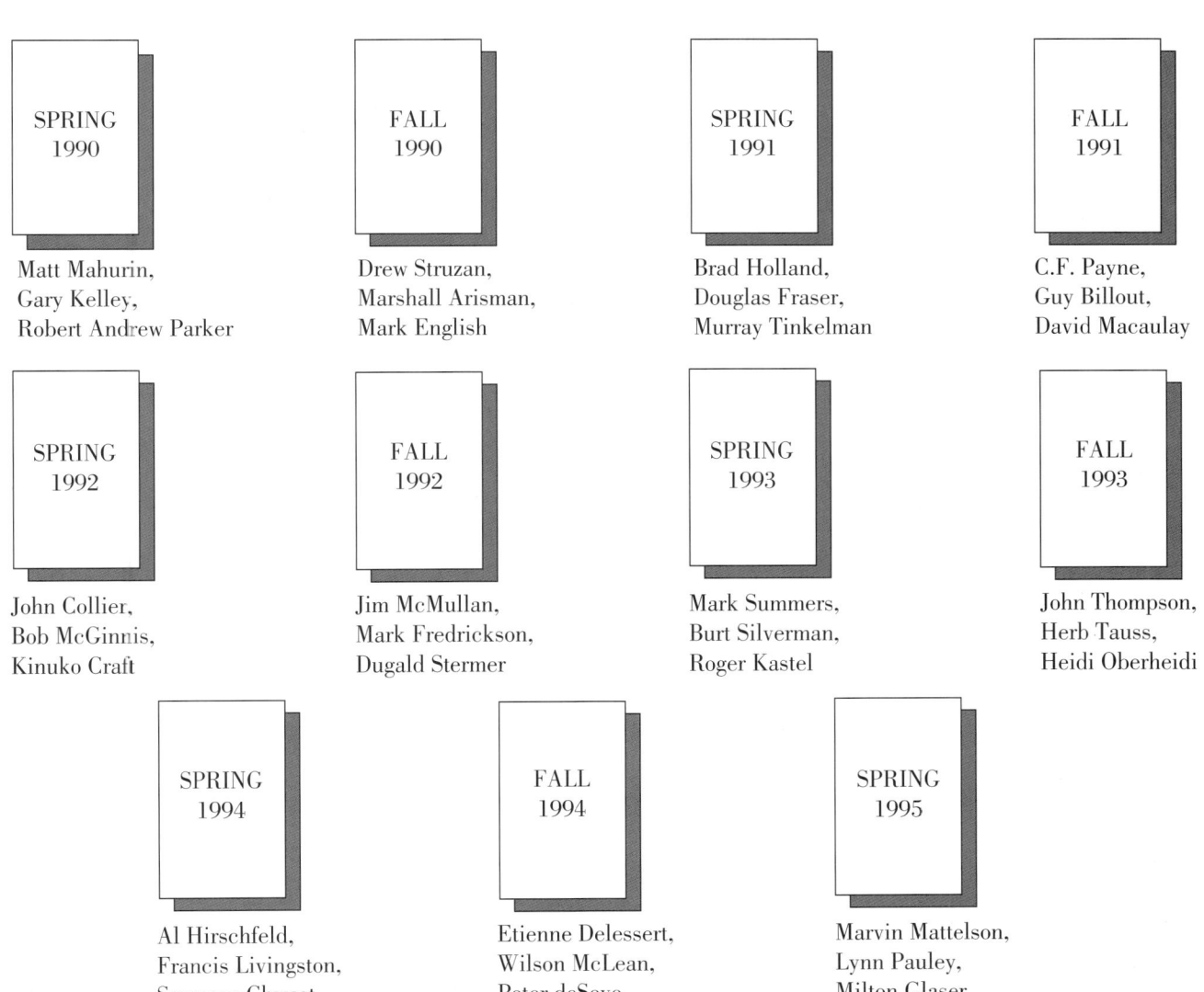

SPRING 1990
Matt Mahurin,
Gary Kelley,
Robert Andrew Parker

FALL 1990
Drew Struzan,
Marshall Arisman,
Mark English

SPRING 1991
Brad Holland,
Douglas Fraser,
Murray Tinkelman

FALL 1991
C.F. Payne,
Guy Billout,
David Macaulay

SPRING 1992
John Collier,
Bob McGinnis,
Kinuko Craft

FALL 1992
Jim McMullan,
Mark Fredrickson,
Dugald Stermer

SPRING 1993
Mark Summers,
Burt Silverman,
Roger Kastel

FALL 1993
John Thompson,
Herb Tauss,
Heidi Oberheidi

SPRING 1994
Al Hirschfeld,
Francis Livingston,
Seymour Chwast

FALL 1994
Etienne Delessert,
Wilson McLean,
Peter deSeve

SPRING 1995
Marvin Mattelson,
Lynn Pauley,
Milton Glaser

For information regarding videotapes of these presentations, for educational use, call 1-800-SIMUSEUM

OUR OWN SHOW 1995

THE SOCIETY OF ILLUSTRATORS MEMBERS SIXTH ANNUAL OPEN EXHIBITION

STEVAN DOHANOS AWARD Leigh Grant

"Our Own Show" is pleased to inaugurate the Stevan Dohanos Award as the Best in Show in this open, unjuried exhibition.

AWARD OF MERIT Jeffrey Fisher

AWARD OF MERIT Maryjane Begin

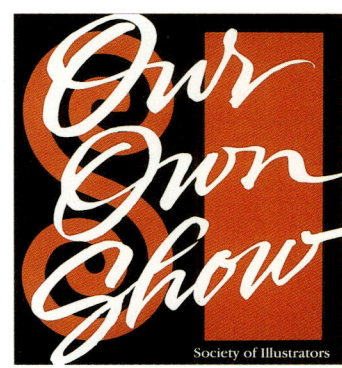

"Our Own Show" was created to extend this annual opportunity for all professionally active members of the Society to exhibit a work in the Museum galleries. Each year nearly 200 artists participate.

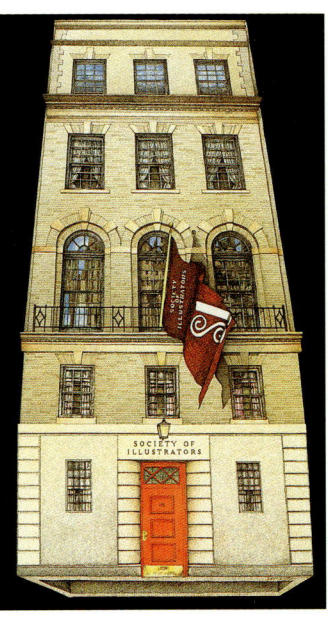

"Our Own Show" is the major funding source for the Ten Year Rebuilding plan which is modernizing the Society's 1875 Carriage House headquarters for the 21st Century.

© 1995, Leigh Grant (203) 846-4577
© 1995 Maryjane Begin (401) 421-2344
© 1995 Jeffrey Fisher (516) 360-3975

SOUNDS FROM THE BULLPEN

BY HOWARD MUNCE

A collection of bleats, bitches & bellyaches anent the calamities & vicissitudes of the minority known as commercial artists.

A collection of outrageous satirical essays about the working life of commercial artists of every stripe. This 80 page, black & white, hard-cover book deals with artists in commerce as they naively tilt at enemy windmills that stretch to the horizon.

This collection was originally written for Bulletin Editor Arpi Ermoyan, for the entertainment and enlightenment of members of the Society of Illustrators and appeared infrequently in the Society's newsletter.

Munce & Webster define "BULL-PEN n. ART as an enclosure where a collection of commercial artists of diverse specialities are corralled like bulls and prisoners in remote and windowless sections of office buildings to keep *them* from rioting. They are kept warmed-up until burnt-out in a game that deals only in emergencies and never progresses. Their seats at their drawing boards become lifelong penalty benches." Munce adds "if this volume has nothing else to recommend it, you will find it just thick enough to stabilize a short-legged table or to urge parents of young people of art school age to sell them to gypsies, enlist them in the Foreign Legion or fast-freeze them until computer graphics take over."

Author Howard Munce is a scarred veteran of 16 years in 6 New York advertising agencies and 30 plus years as a freelance art director, illustrator, and all-around hand and head for hire.

This uniquely, madly written book is for everyone from art student to professional graphics practitioner. It's aimed at all ranks--and all senses of humor. And it is profusely illustrated by the author.

Please send_____ copies of SOUNDS FROM THE BULLPEN at $25.00 plus $5.00 per copy for postage and handling in the United States. Postage and handling to Canada is $9.00, overseas is $15.00. (New York residents add 8 1/4% sales tax.)

MAIL TO: Society of Illustrators, 128 East 63rd Street, New York, NY 10021-7303

Make checks payable to the Society of Illustrators, in United States funds drawn on a United States bank.

Charge my credit card: American Express ❑   Visa ❑   Master Card ❑

Account number:_____   Expiration date:_____

Signature:_____

Print Name:_____

City:_____ State:_____ Zip:_____

You may FAX your credit card order to: (212) 838-2561. Please allow 4 weeks for delivery.

The ILLUSTRATOR IN AMERICA 1880·1980

By Walt & Roger Reed

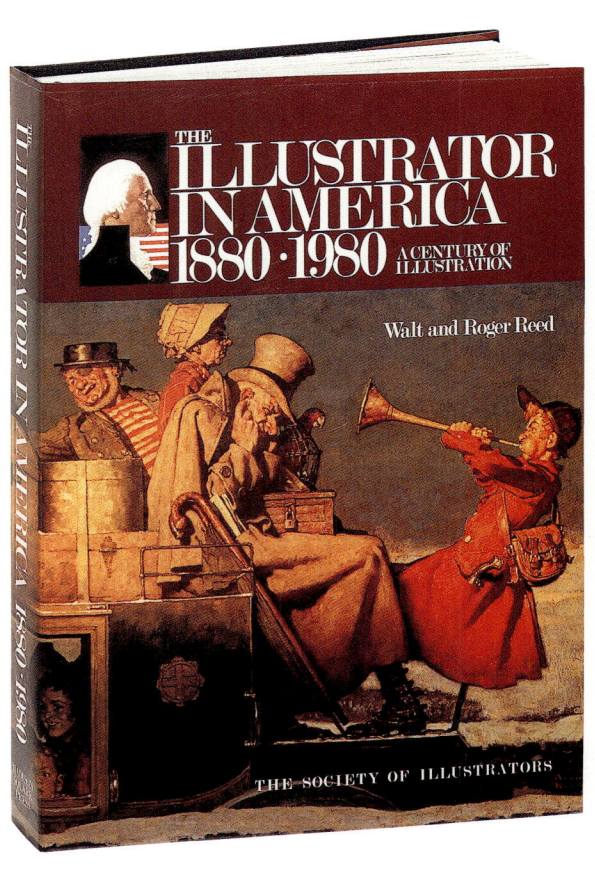

This major reference work of the history of modern illustration includes all the important illustrators, and representations of their work, of the late 19th and 20th centuries. This volume acts as a complete course of this period of American illustration and for this reason is a most valued tool for understanding the history of illustration in this period.

•••

Walt and Roger Reed, respected historians of American illustration, have done a masterful job of selecting the most appropriate images to represent each of the 460 illustrators in this book.

The artists appear in the decade in which their influence was most strongly felt.

Each decade is introduced by a famous illustrator with comprehensive knowledge of the period. Included is a biographical sketch of each of the 460 artists, setting forth all the facts needed to help in the understanding of the artists and their work.

This lavishly produced 9" X 12" 352 page book, containing 700 illustrations, many in full color, by 460 artists is a must for the serious student or collector and a valuable reference for everyone in the profession.

Please send _____ copies of ILLUSTRATOR IN AMERICA 1880/1980 at $48.50 plus $5.00 per copy for postage and handling in the United States. Postage and handling to Canada is $9.00, overseas is $15.00. (New York residents add 8 1/4% sales tax.)

MAIL TO: Society of Illustrators, 128 East 63rd Street, New York, NY 10021-7303

Make checks payable to the Society of Illustrators, in United States funds drawn on a United States bank.

Charge my credit card: American Express ❑   Visa ❑   Master Card ❑

Account number: _____ Expiration date: _____

Signature: _____

Print Name: _____

You may FAX your credit card order to: (212) 838-2561. Please allow 4 weeks for delivery.

SOCIETY of ILLUSTRATORS

ANNUAL EXHIBITION

INTERNATIONAL CATEGORY
DEADLINE: FEBRUARY 1

All published illustrations produced by artists outside the US, for clients outside the US, are invited to submit to the INTERNATIONAL CATEGORY.

Accepted entries will be exhibited in slide form at the Society and reproduced in the next ILLUSTRATORS ANNUAL.

For further information: FAX: 001-121-838-2561 Write: 128 East 63rd Street, New York, NY 10021-7303 USA

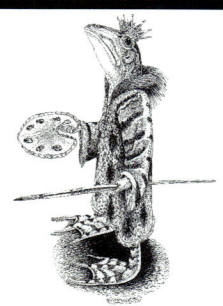

Society of Illustrators
Museum Shop

The Society of Illustrators Museum of American Illustration maintains a shop featuring many quality products. Four-color, large format books document contemporary illustration and the great artists of the past. Museum quality prints and posters capture classic images. T-shirts, sweatshirts, hats, mugs and tote bags make practical and fun gifts.

The Museum Shop is an extension of the Society's role as the center for illustration in America today. For further information or quantity discounts, contact the Society at TEL: (212) 838-2560 / FAX: (212) 838-2561

NEW!
ILLUSTRATORS 37
352pp. Cover by Gary Kelley. Contains the 452 works accepted by the juries. Also the 56 works accepted in the new International Category. Hall of Fame, Hamilton King Awards. The most contemporary look at Illustration worldwide.
$57.50

ILLUSTRATORS ANNUAL BOOKS

These catalogs are based on our annual juried exhibitions, divided into four major categories in American Illustration: Editorial, Book, Advertising, and Institutional. Some are available in a limited supply only.

In addition, a limited number of out-of-print collector's editions of the Illustrators Annuals that are not listed above (1959 to Illustrators 30) are available as is.

Also available for collectors are back issues of The Art Directors Club annuals and GRAPHIS Annuals.

Contact the Society for details...

SOCIETY OF ILLUSTRATORS • 128 East 63rd Street • New York, NY 10021

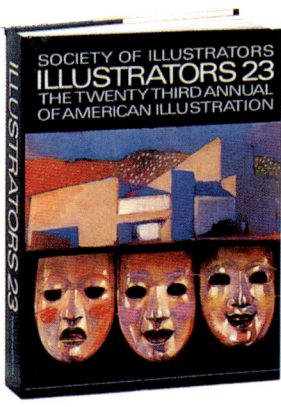
ILLUSTRATORS 23
$20.00
limited number remaining

ILLUSTRATORS 24
$20.00
limited number remaining

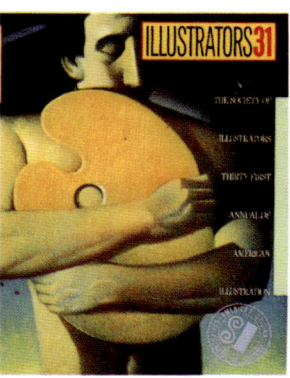
ILLUSTRATORS 31
$40.00
limited number remaining

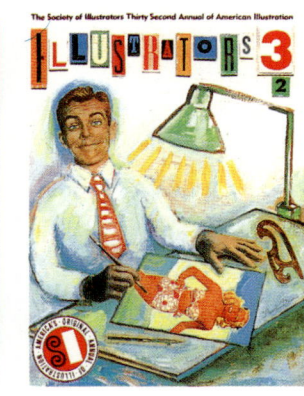
ILLUSTRATORS 32
$45.00

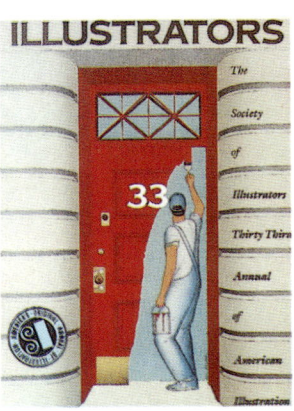
ILLUSTRATORS 33
$45.00

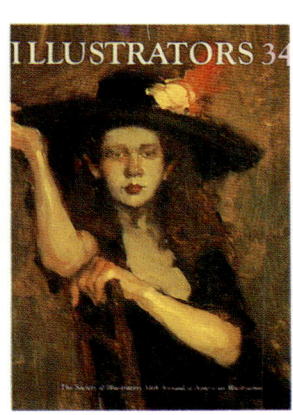
ILLUSTRATORS 34
$45.00

ILLUSTRATORS 35
$49.95

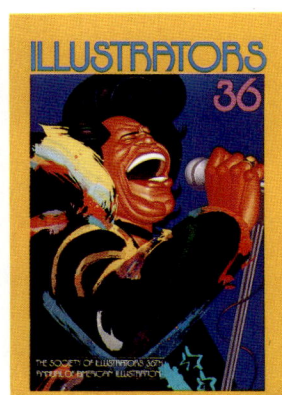
ILLUSTRATORS 36
$57.00

ART FOR SURVIVAL
248 pp, full color, 150 images by contemporary illustrators commenting on the Environment. Introductions by Tom Cruise and others. $40.00

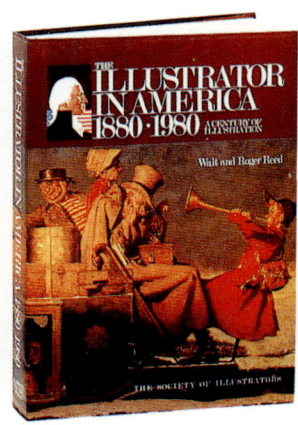
THE ILLUSTRATOR IN AMERICA (1880-1980) -355 pp. Compiled by leading authorities on illustration. Contains 700 illustrations by 460 artists. $40.00

Dean Cornwell, "Gold Hands", Cosmopolitan, 1923
$12.00

Joseph Christian Leyendecker,"Easter" The Saturday Evening Post, 1935 © Curtis Publishing 1935 $12.00

Mead Schaeffer, "Stagecoach Holdup" The American Magazine, 1937
$12.00

MUSEUM QUALITY POSTERS

Posters of classic works from the Society's permanent collection. Reproduced on glossy stock in a 20" x 30" format.
Suitable for framing. $12.00 per poster; $38.00 for the set of four.

N.C. Wyeth,"The Black Arrow" by Robert Louis Stevenson Charles Scribner's Sons, 1916 $12.00

EXHIBITION POSTERS

Posters created for exhibitions in the Society of Illustrators Museum of American Illustration. Suitable for framing. $10.00 per poster; $27.00 for the set of three.

"Recycled Ideas"
"The Illustrator and the Environment"
by FOLON $10.00

"Science Fiction" by JOHN BERKEY, 1984
$10.00

"Wizard of Oz", The Original Art by EDWARD SOREL, 1991
$10.00

UNIQUE EDITION

150 pages in full color of Children's books from 1992. This volume contains valuable "how-to" comments from the artists as well as a publishers directory. A compilation of the exhibition, "The Original Art 1992 - Celebrating the Fine Art of Children's Book Illustration."
$29.95

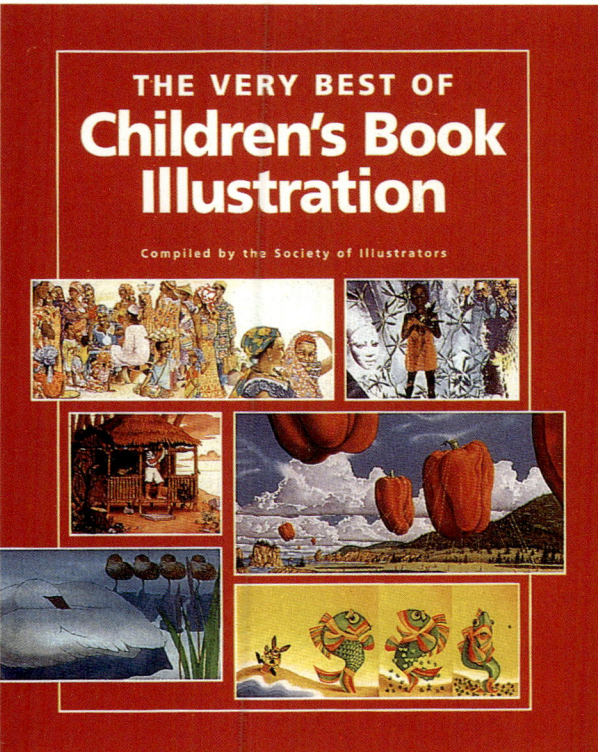

"The 34th Annual Exhibition", by Brad Holland, 1992
$10.00

THE BUSINESS LIBRARY

Each of thesee volumes is a valuable asset to the professional artist whether established or just starting out. Together they form a solid base for your business.

The set of three volumes. $42.00

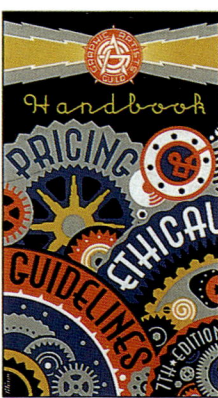 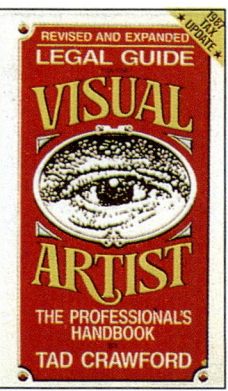 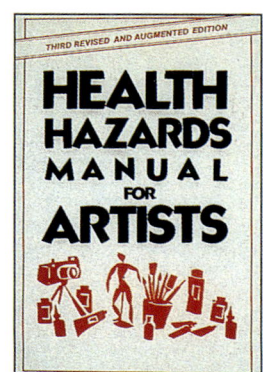

GRAPHIC ARTISTS GUILD HANDBOOK PRICING AND ETHICAL GUIDELINES - Vol. 7
Includes an outline of ethical standards and business practices, as well as price ranges for hundreds of uses and sample contracts.
$22.95

THE LEGAL GUIDE FOR THE VISUAL ARTIST 1994 Edition.
Tad Crawford's text explains basic copyrights, moral rights, the sale of rights, taxation, business accounting and the legal support groups available to artists.
$18.95

HEALTH HAZARDS MANUAL
A comprehensive review of materials and supplies, from fixatives to pigments, airbrushes to solvents.
$9.95

GIFT ITEMS

The Society's famous Red and Black logo, designed by Bradbury Thompson, is featured on the following gift items:

SI BASEBALL CAPS
Blue or red corduroy, adjustable back strap and the logo in white
$15.00

SI LAPEL PINS
$6.00
Actual Size

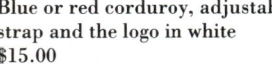

SI PATCH
White with blue lettering and piping - 4" wide
$4.00

SI TOTE BAGS
Heavyweight, white canvas bags are 14" high with the two-color logo
$15.00

SI CERAMIC COFFEE MUGS
Heavyweight 14 oz. mugs are white with the two-color logo
$6.00 each, $20.00 for a set of 4

SI T-SHIRTS

Incorporating the Society's 1962 logo by Bradbury Thompson. White, heavy cotton shirt with two-color logo.
$10.00 each
Sizes: Small, Large, X-Large, XX-Large

SI SWEATSHIRTS

Blue with white lettering of multiple logos. Grey with large red SI.
$20.00 each.
Sizes:
Large,
X-Large,
XX-Large.

SI NOTE CARDS

Norman Rockwell greeting cards, 3-7/8" x 8-5/8", inside blank, great for all occasions. Includes 100% rag envelopes

10 cards - $10.00
20 cards - $18.00
50 cards - $35.00
100 cards - $60.00

ORDER FORM
Mail to the attention of:
The Museum Shop, SOCIETY OF ILLUSTRATORS, 128 East 63rd Street, New York, NY 10021

NAME _____

COMPANY _____

STREET _____

CITY _____

STATE _____ ZIP _____

DAYTIME PHONE ( ) _____

Enclosed is my check for $ _____
Make checks payable to Society of Illustrators
Please charge my credit card:
❏ American Express   ❏ Master Card   ❏ Visa
Card Number _____
Signature _____ Expiration Date _____
*please note if name appearing on the card is different than the mailing name.

Qty	Description	Size	Color	Price	Total
# of items ordered		Total price of item(s) ordered			
		*Shipping/handling per order			3.50
				TOTAL DUE	

*Foreign postage additional

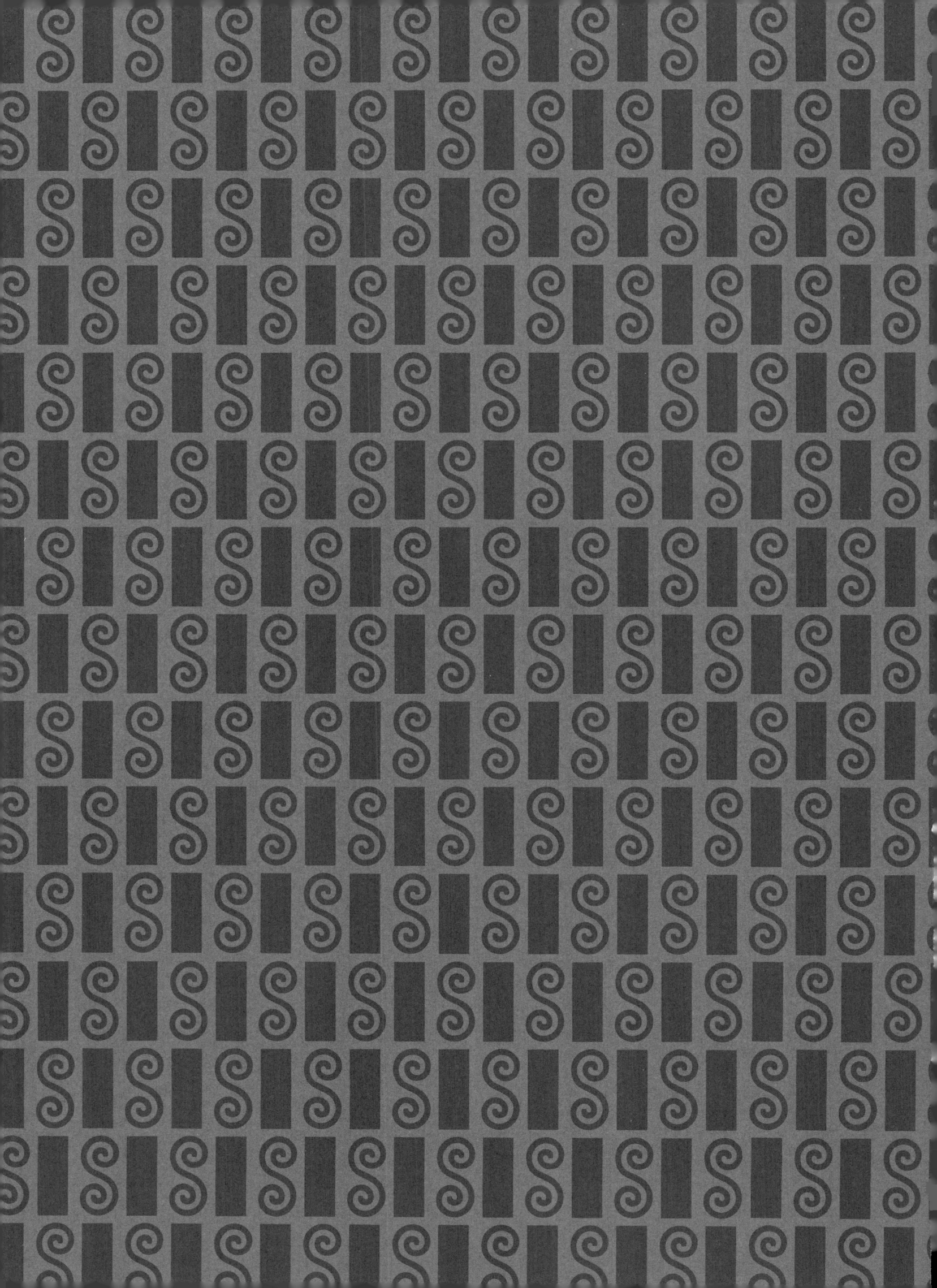